William Anderson Scott

The Centurions of the Gospel

William Anderson Scott

The Centurions of the Gospel

ISBN/EAN: 9783337308636

Printed in Europe, USA, Canada, Australia, Japan

Cover: Foto ©Lupo / pixelio.de

More available books at **www.hansebooks.com**

THE CENTURIONS OF THE GOSPEL:

WITH DISCOURSES ON

"THE CHOICE OF A PROFESSION," "OUR RESPONSIBILITY FOR OUR FELLOW MEN," AND THE "PIETY AND PATRIOTISM OF PRAYING FOR OUR RULERS."

BY

REV. W. A. SCOTT, D. D.,

PASTOR OF THE FORTY-SECOND STREET PRESBYTERIAN CHURCH, NEW YORK.

SECOND EDITION.

NEW YORK:
ANSON D. F. RANDOLPH,
710 BROADWAY.
1868.

Entered according to Act of Congress, in the year 1867,

By REV. W. A. SCOTT, D. D.,

In the Clerk's Office of the District Court of the United States for the Southern District of New York.

PREFACE.

A NEW edition of the following Discourses being called for, it has seemed best to change the title from "The Church in the Army; or the Four Centurions," to one that expresses more satisfactorily the nature of the volume. The aim of these Discourses is, to show that the Gospel is suited for all sorts of men in all the circumstances of life. The *Four Centurions* are selected as examples from the military profession, and the other Discourses are an attempt to illustrate great Bible principles, and teach lessons and inculcate duties which are of the greatest importance in all the callings or pursuits of life, however humble or exalted, and in our judgment lie essentially at the very foundation of all true happiness here and hereafter.

It is believed there never was a time, since the foundation of the world, when there was so much zeal displayed for supplying soldiers, marines, sailors, merchants, and travellers, with religious books as at the present moment. It is well. For never was there a time when the great nations of the earth were making such rapid strides in material progress and wealth, as they are doing in our day. Never was there so much intelligent *immortal* mind employed in secular callings,—never was there a greater propriety or necessity for our sea-going men and soldiers, and merchants and travellers, to be proper representatives of our holy religion in the face of heathen peoples and around the globe as in our day. For "their line is gone out through all the earth, and their words to the end of the world. There is no speech nor language, where their voice is not heard."

Generations before us, it is true, were not altogether indifferent to such subjects. Not a few names are known, that the Christian world "will not willingly let die"—famous for enterprise, skill, courage, and success in life, and equally renowned for their piety. *Cromwell*, though he lived in the days of storm and tempest, ordered a pocket-bible to be prepared (1643) for his armies, which was called "The Soldiers' Bible." The heading of this bible has these lines:

> "A SOULDIER MUST NOT DOE WICKEDLY:
> A SOULDIER MUST BE VALIANT FOR GOD'S SAKE·
> A SOULDIER MUST PRAY BEFORE HE GO TO FIGHT."

This bible was generally buttoned between the coat and the vest, next the soldier's heart. One of the elders of the First Presbyterian Church of New Orleans, of which I had the honor to be pastor for a number of years, has a pocket-bible, which he found thus on the breast of a Highland soldier, who fell on the battle-field of the eighth of January, before New Orleans. It bears the marks of long use, and of the deadly conflict. And it is hoped its former owner had so understood and applied its precious truths, that he went home from Chalmette's ensanguined plains to the better land, "where Peace eternal reigns."

Many volumes and legions of tracts and ballads have been recently published, on the patriotism, heroism, and piety of Christian soldiers. The Discourses contained in this volume were all prepared, and some of them published, several years before our Civil War, which is now, thanks be to God! ended and numbered with the things that are passed. There is, consequently, no allusion in this volume to any thing connected with our late war.

In the opinion of some intelligent and thoughtful and pious men, much of the popular religious literature of our day is lamentably wanting in devotion and elegance of style. As a whole, it is not up to the standard of literary excellence found in our secular works. One of the wonders of our day of telegraphs and steamships is the able and fine writing of our Daily and our Weekly publications, which are fast superseding the *Monthlies*, as they have, in some measure, superseded the stately *Quarterlies*. And surely if our children are ever to become vigorous Christians of a full stature in Christ Jesus, they must have the Divine Word to nourish their souls, and not be required to grow up always upon the *namby-pamby* of childish stories, even if they are not altogether works of fiction. It is well known that many thoughtful persons among us fear that a considerable portion of our popular religious publications are of a sickly tendency, and will not produce the desired impression upon the minds of our liberally educated young people, especially of the learned professions. The fear is that there is too much *pietism* or *cant* in them for men so intelligent as are generally found in the Civil service, or in the Army and Navy. It is within the writer's personal knowledge that officers of our Army have felt aggrieved by seeing the records of private feelings and of religious experience *published* from letters and journals that were never written with any thought of their publication. They have said, after looking over such works: "If this is the piety of soldiers, and the way it is to be regarded, we want none of it." It is, therefore, with great pleasure we are able to say that the biographical sketches of General Havelock, that have fallen under our observation, are of a decidedly healthful and *manly* tone. He was "every inch a soldier and every inch a Christian." No man in the British Army possessed more common sense, persevering mental application, or greater moral and physical courage. His life seems to us likely to make a favorable impression on the Army and Navy, and on the educated young men of our day generally. We like it just for the same reason that we would have our Sabbath-school children earnestly engaged in committing the Creed, the Ten Commandments, the Lord's Prayer, the Psalms, and the Gospel of John, to memory, rather than that they should distract and weaken their tender minds, by fictions and the *hot-house* literature that it is so much the fashion of our day to "cram" into our Sunday-schools. We can, however, recommend, and with much confidence, such works as the "Life of Havelock," Cecil's "Remains," Scott's "Force of Truth," Wilberforce's "Practical View," Henry's "Anxious Inquirer," and Dr. A. Alexander's "Thoughts on Religious Experience."

It will be seen in the course of this volume also, that the author had an intimate acquaintance with the habits and sentiments of *General Andrew Jackson*, of Tennessee, being his Pastor for some years after he retired from Washington, and that he believes he was "the most religious President we have ever had."

This volume is a labor of love. Born amid the scenes of frontier life, and familiar with Indian wars from youth, and having considerable knowledge of the American Army, and having many personal friends among its officers, this work has been long meditated by the author. One of his earliest friends, whose name is embalmed in his heart, is an officer in the Army. We have known him now for a lifetime, until he is near the head of his profession, and we hesitate not to say, that he is one of the most consistently pious and intelligent men we have ever known. But as he yet lives to adorn his profession, we forbear to publish his name, for we know that his feelings are as delicate as his courage is exalted. We remember distinctly his religious habits in the camp and in the barracks. We know that it was his custom, whenever circumstances would at all permit it, to read a chapter every day in the Bible, with Dr. Thomas Scott's notes, and to write out a synopsis of them; and on the Lord's day, if no chaplain was present, he conducted a religious service for his men.

In these Discourses, I have not sought novelties, but to present the Truth, which is in order to salvation as it lies in the brief histories under examination. After years of thought and reading, it is not easy to analyze one's store of knowledge, and name with absolute accuracy the writers to whom we may be indebted, in one way or another, for facts and illustrations. I have consulted with some diligence, and, as far as I deemed it needful for my purpose, have exhausted such commentators in French, Latin, and Greek, and partially in German, as well as in English, as I have had access to, or have considered worth the time required for studying them. The historical facts of the volume are taken from most reliable sources, and I hope will be found to be correct. It is, also, but justice to say, that while the authors and commentaries on the Scriptures, whom I have designed to honor in this acknowledgment just made, or made in the progress of the volume itself, have embraced the lives of the warriors of the Bible, and have presented quite extensive notes on the FOUR CENTURIONS, of whose conversion we have some account, as I think, in the New Testament; still, as far as my information extends, there is no work like this volume—*no work that attempts to give a commentary, on the character and conversion to Christ of the Roman Centurions, as written for us by the sacred penmen, illustrated by reference to the lives of pious men in the military profession of modern times.*

The author's great aim in gratefully recording the power of the Gospel, and making mention of the evidences of true piety, furnished by the Centurions, and by soldiers of more recent times, is to awaken in the breasts of his young countrymen the conviction, that eminent piety is not a real hindrance to success, in any of the honorable pursuits of life, but is a decided advantage in them all, and that even in the military profession, it is a Bible truth, that true religion is the way to make "*the best of both worlds.*" His prayer for young men, seeing "they are strong," is that they may be "as plants of the Lord, grown up in their youth," and it is only the more earnest, because the times are evil, and the night of death approaches when no man can work.

W. A. SCOTT.

NEW YORK, *December*, 1867.

CONTENTS.

                                                        PAGE

INTRODUCTION 19

Ruskin's prophecy—"Sons of war" may be subjects of "the Prince of Peace," when war is justifiable, which is rarely the case—Rev. Mr. Boardman's "Higher Life"—General Halleck's answer to Dr. Wayland—John the Baptist style of John Knox—*The Gospel is Peace.*

I.—THE CENTURION OF CAPERNAUM 25

1. *The Coming to Jesus.*—The time of this miracle—The scene of it—The site of Capernaum—Fate of the city—The Centurion was a Roman officer—Why he came to Jesus—Matthew and Luke reconciled—Proverbial liberality of soldiers and sailors—The sick "servant"—His disease.

II.—THE CENTURION OF CAPERNAUM CONTINUED 38

2. *The peculiar Excellence of his Faith.*—Our Lord's prompt reply to the call for help—We must trust our senses—Faith, what is it?—Our Lord's wonder at the greatness of the Centurion's faith—How it was distinguished—He had been brought up in heathenism—He was a soldier—The military profession has given many illustrious examples of piety—Havelock.

III.—THE CENTURION OF CAPERNAUM CONTINUED 49

3. *Evidences of this Centurion's Faith.*—Was kind to his servant—Remarkable completeness of this soldier's character—Reformation not always a true conversion—"*Havelock's saints*" Christianity is not built out of the ruins of humanity, manhood or civilization—Insubordination a crying evil in our day—The Centurion's remarkable humility: "I am not worthy"—Did not assume with Anglo-Saxon-like pride to be better than any other people—He makes a true soldier's brief, prompt profession of his faith—Mistaken ideas of true manliness or independence of character—Nothing "fawning" or corrupt in this soldier's humility—Our Lord not only granted his request, but entered into his heart—His faith distinguished for its independence of the senses—And also because it disregarded his

Roman prejudices against the Jews—His faith assumed a military form.

IV.—THE CENTURION OF CAPERNAUM CONTINUED................ 69
4. *This Roman officer still preaching the Gospel.*—*First*, here we have our Lord's perfect humanity—*Secondly*, we should not indulge in general and indiscriminating charges upon classes and professions, races or callings—Not necessary for soldiers and sailors to swear, even if the *Army in Flanders* did—Havelock's example—His prayer-meeting in the heathen temple of Shivey Dagoon—A picture wanted of his Rangoon pagoda—Lord Bentick's testimony in favor of Havelock and his "saints"—Some professions are more favorable than others, but none are excused from being pious—Peter no doubt a saint in heaven, whether he was a pope or not—Arnold's treachery does not prove WASHINGTON a hypocrite—*Thirdly*, let us be more charitable—The Gospel kingdom is open to all nations—*Fourthly*, this miracle a clear reality—*Fifthly*, disadvantages enhance the value of success—*Sixthly*, our Lord estimates a man according to his faith—*Seventhly*, natural for the Centurion's faith to run in the channel of his profession—His military science taught him faith in an invisible presence—So the "wise men" and the "shepherds" were led to Christ in their own calling—*The business by which we make our living in this world should educate us at the same time for heaven*—Wonderful condescension and wisdom in the means by which we are taught the goodness of God—"The crawling beetle" and "the desert moss"—*Eighthly*, faith instantaneous—Have you received the Almighty Saviour as the Roman soldier did?

V.—THE CENTURION COMMANDING AT THE CRUCIFIXION........ 91
This centurion's position enabled him to give a remarkable testimony—His company unite with him—meaning of his words, "Truly this man was the Son of God"—No contradiction in our narratives—"Son of God" critically examined—"Filius Dei" all a Roman could say—The Roman officer certainly meant to decide in favor of Jesus as against the Jews—Remarkable circumstances under which his testimony is given—It is in direct opposition to the verdict of the Sanhedrim, Syna-

gogue and mob—Soldiers and sailors remarkable for quickness of apprehension and correctness of sight—Calvin's idea about the Centurion's conversion—Unconscious prophesyings "glorified God"—Concurring events that attended the Centurion's testimony—Was he not embraced in our Lord's dying prayer?—Meaning of "Certainly this was a righteous man"—Jesus, though crucified under a judicial sentence was a *righteous man*—Pilate, and Pilate's wife, and Herod, and even Judas himself, unite in the Centurion's testimony, He was a *righteous man*—HIS RIGHTEOUSNESS IS OUR SALVATION—The divine portrait presents us with an Almighty Redeemer—Proof that Jesus was the Son of God—The history condensed—Contrary effects of evidence upon men caused by their prejudices—Our rock is not as their rock, even our enemies being judges.

VI.—THE CENTURION OF CESAREA........ 125

1. *The subject of Divine Grace here introduced.*—His name Cornelius—His residence—Cesarea, ancient and modern—"The Italian band" illustrated, "The New York regiment," or "Louisiana Legion"—Historic proof—Cornelius was a perfect gentleman as well as a highly accomplished soldier—He feared God, gave alms and was religious in his household—"Feared God," yet was not an Israelite, nor even a proselyte—"And prayed to God always"—Official rank and soldier-like habits are not inconsistent with piety—Graveyards and nearness to churches do not sanctify—Plagues in cities have not converted them—Opportunities always found for sinning, when they are sought.

VII.—THE CENTURION OF CESAREA CONTINUED............. 138

2. *The means used for his Conversion.*—When was he "effectually called"—Process of conviction—Means used for his conversion to Christ—His vision—God's angel—"For a memorial"—Joppa—"Simon the tanner"—Peter's trance—Cornelius' character declared to Peter—Peter's hospitality—His companions to Cesarea—Peter's example for zeal and fidelity—Union of personal and relative duties in this Roman soldier—Sunday school teachers and parents admonished and encouraged—Union of piety and morality as seen in this Centurion—The eminence of his piety—His benevolence—No controversy between good works

and salvation by Grace—The self-righteous and vain moralist condemned by Cornelius—The Gospel offer is universal.

VIII.—THE CENTURION OF CESAREA CONTINUED............ 166
3. *Peter's Sermon on the occasion of his Conversion.*—Gentile converts received into the Christian church—Olshausen and Prof. J. A. Alexander on his religious status—His history recited—Means employed to make CHRIST known to him—Peter's sheet a symbol—*Peter's sermon:* 1st. God no respecter of persons—Bengel—All religions are not equally good—Peter did not invent, but then discovered God's universal regard for all nations—2d. Peter's sermon was original and expository—" Witnesses chosen before God " were competent and the best in every respect—We must believe upon testimony—3d. Jesus is the Messiah according to all the prophets—Ministers are to preach this, and nothing else—4th. The Holy Ghost confirmed Peter's preaching—The baptism of the Holy Ghost and of water—*Lessons*, 1. The self-denial of the apostles—2. Proof of the power of Divine grace on a Roman soldier—God's Word honored—The Gospel must be preached not by angels, but by men—3. Procuring cause is not to be confounded with the evidence or fruit of this man's faith—4. Observe the *moral courage* of this Roman officer—Moral courage the great want of our evil times—Have you courage to do right? Have you courage to profess Christ?

IX.—PAUL'S VOYAGE AND SHIPWRECK...... 197
Julius the Centurion in command of the prisoners from Judea to Rome—The course of the voyage from Cesarea—The tempest —The fasting—Paul's vision—His courage and influence on the crew—The wreck—Melita, the barbarians—Paul's miracle and preaching—Subsequent voyage and arrival at Rome—His labors and preaching in the Eternal City.

X.—JULIUS, THE CENTURION OF PAUL'S VOYAGE TO ROME....... 307
Melita is Malta—Ships and navigation of the ancients—Occasion of Paul's voyage—His companions—The Centurion Julius compared with the three others we have had in the sacred history —Christ's word blessed when uttered by his disciples—Julius' first acquaintance with his illustrious prisoner—Paul's bearing in the hour of danger—The Centurion's interference to save

the prisoners for Paul's sake—Why did the Centurion take such an interest in the Hebrew prisoner?—The Roman centurion's character—His band was the *Cohors Augusta*—Lepsius—The Centurion's observation of Paul—His opportunities to form a correct opinion concerning him—The course of the voyage historically correct—Lardiner in proof—The difference between Paul and the owner and master of the ship as to what was to be done in the tempest—Paul a better mariner than they—The failure—The boat taken up like a Mississippi yawl—" Undergirding " the ship—Lord Anson quoted—Nautical phrases used—Paul's vision—Divine interposition at the time of extremity—Paul was not deceived—He was jealous for God's honor—His great influence—" True courage makes one a majority "—1. Observe the accuracy of Paul's prediction—2. Paul's conversion a proof of the truth of Christianity—His own account of it must have made a deep impression upon this Roman officer—3. God is sovereign and man free—Burkitt's illustration of this—4. Benefit of being in good company—The other prisoners and all the crew saved for Paul's sake—5. Was this Roman Centurion converted to Christ?—6. Deliverances from the perils of battle, or from the dangers of a sea voyage, call for special thanksgivings—7. Difficulties should not discourage us—Joseph—The Hebrew orphan queen of Persia—Paul in Rome—" Across the river."

XI.—THE CHOICE OF A CALLING OR PROFESSION 241
The things essential for our chief end—Life a battle and death a victory—General Jackson's motto—The brave never die—We have a right to ask God what he would have us do—He will guide us as to a business in life—Paul's case illustrates general principles for us—Paul arrives in Damascus in a very different frame of mind from the one with which he set out—Principle should determine what kind of a business we are to follow—Circumstances unlooked for—Sir Walter Scott—Joseph, the son of Jacob.—1. Seek to know the will of God as to what calling you are to follow—How to ascertain what the will of God is—Personal piety the first requisite—Careful examination recommended—Consult your own conscience—A delicate and vastly important concern—Strive for a good conscience—Cases

of warning—Saul of Tarsus and the Jews in crucifying our Lord—See whether you have courage and strength for the business or profession you propose to follow—Granite men wanted—The clipper that has outbraved the tempest—Public opinion, how important, irresistible, yet tyrannical—Individual responsibility—Dr. Wayland's secret of success—*Hold on to the right and the heavens cannot fall*—2. Consider what special qualifications you have for this or that business—A glance at agriculture—Biblical instances of divine teaching in the ordinary arts—Every man is made on a great life plan—Napoleon, Wellington, Jackson, Havelock—Moses Stuart—3. Choose a business by which you may be useful—Art, fine arts and manufacturing—All agree—BREAD IS KING—Mechanical pursuits—Medical profession—Legal profession—The teacher—Associative toil is man's strength—Ruskin on avarice—Enthusiasm in your calling essential to success—God's rule is, that man must labor under constraint of law—Eminence is within your reach—The place of the Gospel in the world—4. Follow the intimations of Providence—Early religious training—General Jackson's mother—Havelock's early religious instruction—Take care of your health—A lawyer's case—Look well at the circumstances of your place and times—Great loss sustained by not following providential allotments—Christians are called to do better than others, even in the humblest callings—Our youth are precocious, conceited—Look at the moral tendency of the business you are about to choose—Measure the strength of the opposition you will meet—Have a regard to the recompense—The rule is that we are to be rewarded according to our labors, and not according to our success—Moses—Paul—Dr. Van Rensselaer's report—The " CROWN ROOM."

XII.—OUR RESPONSIBILITY FOR THE SALVATION OF OUR FELLOW MEN 304

Daniel Webster on responsibility—Omission of duty is guilt—The Mishna's illustration—Cases in point—Egyptians—Men are prone to excuses for neglecting the salvation of their fellow men—God does not accept such excuses—He ponders the heart and considereth our ways—1. Our fellow men are in danger—" Drawn into death—ready to be slain "—The slaying of the soul, what it is—Men are in danger because they are sinning against God—Sin is a dreadful contagion—A man's creed as well as his practice is important—Nor does sincerity in error excuse us from its guilt—2. All our excuses are in vain—We do know, or should know, the danger our fellow-men are in—Nor are we excused from some anxiety about their welfare—Ministers not alone in their responsibility—*Pearls before swine* misapplied—We are our brother's keeper—The means are to be provided, and then everything done we can do, according to God's own appointed ways, to make them effectual—Case of savage nations illustrated—3. Reasons why we should strive to save our fellow men— Our own experience—We all have influence—If converted to God they are happy—This is the way also to promote our own happiness—Great efforts called for in behalf of our new States and cities, and for our soldiers and sea-going men.

REFLECTIONS.

1. Have we realized what it is for a soul to be saved or lost?—2. If our fellow men now perish, it will be after the most precious provisions have been made for their salvation—3. It is something to us that they are ready to be slain—We are under tremendous obligations—Parents, teachers, officers appealed to.

XIII.—THE PIETY AND PATRIOTISM OF PRAYING FOR OUR CIVIL RULERS 351
Political fathers under the same rule as our spiritual and natural fathers—The apostle's teaching on this subject—God still Supreme Governor—True religion the basis of all order and virtue—men prone to extremes—No union of Christ with Cæsar—The powers that be are ordained of God—Illustrations—It is an act of true patriotism and of the most disinterested loyalty to pray for our civil rulers—Hebrews and early Christians did so—Fear of God and a proper regard for man are found together—Good rulers desire the prayers of the pious—The Church of God has always taught and practised this duty—Various authorities cited from Barrow, Chrysostom, Origen and others—The Catechism teaches it—Common charity requires

it—The human prone to carry us astray—Our civil rulers need our sympathy and prayers—Their post is difficult and dangerous—They are a part of ourselves—Our welfare depends upon them—Prayer is an essential part of every man's piety.

XIV.—CHRISTIAN SOLDIERS............................. 395
Colonel Gardiner—His bravery, patriotism, piety and death—Captain Vicars—His activity as a Christian, noble bearing in battle and death at Sebastopol—Marshal Suwarrow—Russia's greatest general—His heroism, devotion and influence over his soldiers—General Havelock—Sum of his character as a soldier and Christian—Long waiting for his work—Well done at last—His victories Diligence in acquiring knowledge—A noble example for young officers—The military profession not in itself sinful—Havelock's character and Christian death—General Jackson—Pliny's remark—Author's opportunity to study his character—Walpole's rule a failure—General Jackson's moral courage and estimate of it in public men—His attainments—His letters—Devotion to his friends—His early religious education—Never altogether lost—Becomes a communing church member—The author his pastor at the Hermitage—His attendance at the Lord's supper—Judge Gayarré's sketch—Difficulty of doing justice to his memory—Cobbett's estimate of General Jackson—His fame will grow greener in coming years—Oft allusions to the help of Providence—His habit of reading the Bible—His pious reflections on the death of a friend and his own failing health—Dr. Esselman's letter describing his death—The closing scene.

XV.—THE ARMY OF THE DEAD STILL SPEAKING,............. 425
The holy catholic Church—Every age and generation connected—Aim of this volume—All great men pious—Illustrations from Homer's heroes—God works by fit agents—Alexander's love for the *Iliad*—Domestic purity and attachment not inconsistent with the loftiest heroism—The Centurions—Havelock—Jackson—Such men are to be imitated—Faith in Christ necessary—Our religion must be confessed—Soldiers must try to do good—Catholicity of feeling characteristic of brave men—Havelock not a close communionist—Unfavorable circumstances may be overcome—Conclusion.

INTRODUCTION

SOLDIERS MAY BE PIOUS.

"Every inch a soldier and every inch a Christian."—LORD HARDINGE'S EULOGY ON GEN. HAVELOCK.

From an intimate acquaintance with General Jackson's habits and sentiments, I have no doubt the Rev. Dr. Wilson was correct in saying, that "General Jackson, though not a regular professor of religion while acting President, was, however, the most religious President we have ever had."—THE AUTHOR.

"For many a year to come, the sword of every righteous nation must be whetted to save or to subdue; nor will it be by patience of others' suffering, but by the offering of your own, that you will ever draw nearer to the time when the great change shall pass upon the iron of the earth; when men shall beat their swords into ploughshares, and their spears into pruning hooks; neither shall they learn war any more."*

If Mr. Ruskin is correct, war is to be the trade of man for ages to come. Alas, alas! that it should be so. But since it is so, and has been so from the beginning, and we fear will so continue for ages to come, it is proper for us to consider briefly the question:

Can the son of war, be a child of God? Is it possible for a man of blood to be a sincere follower of the Prince of Peace? Various observations and facts are given in this volume as illustrations of what kind of an answer should be given to this question. Historically, we know that neither the exclusive

---

* Ruskin's Lectures, p. 250.

divine right of kings, nor the doctrine of passive obedience and non-resistance even to tyranny, has been able to prevent wars in past ages. And until human nature shall be vastly changed from what it is, we do not see that wars will cease out of the earth. And as long as wars exist, so long will there be soldiers. Whether war is the natural state of man or not, certain it is, that as it has been, so it is now, and so it will be to the end of our present economy. Does Christianity then absolutely forbid all wars? Is it impossible for a Christian man to engage in war without violating his principles? That most wars are unlawful and wholly unjustifiable, we are ready to admit. But all wars are not alike. Peace and war are noble or otherwise, according to their kind and occasion. And even as to wicked and unholy wars, are not tax-payers just as much involved in their sinfulness as the officers and men of the army and navy that are actually engaged in carrying them on? And if all wars are sinful, how is it that God himself ever commanded his chosen people to go to war?

Jehovah is never so straitened for means to carry forward his purposes as to do evil that good may come out of it. Never. And moreover, if war is always and essentially a moral wrong, how are we to look upon the wars of Abraham, Joshua, Gideon, Moses and David? And what are we to say of the acknowledged piety of Vicars, Hammond, Col. Gardiner, Gen. Burns, the Lawrences, Nicholsons, Edwardes, and General Havelock, and many others in modern times living and dead, who are ornaments and pillars of the Church of God, and yet at the same time are distinguished for their service to their country in the army and navy?

Nor do we find in the New Testament any censure upon the centurions whose history is presented in the following pages, for their connection with the military profession. There is not a syllable like this recorded of the centurion of Capernaum, nor of Cornelius, nor of the centurion in command at the crucifixion, nor of Julius, who had charge of Paul on his perilous journey to Rome. Nor did John the Baptist, nor our Lord in preaching to soldiers, intimate that their profession was inconsistent with the ethics of Christianity. And besides this presumptive testimony against the objection, that a military man cannot be a good Christian, what is the army or the navy but a national police? If it is right for a city to have its mayor, sheriff, constables and police, then it is right for a nation to have its army and navy. They are nothing but its police force to suppress insurrection, enforce law and preserve order. Laws without penalties are no laws at all. Then every man must be his own judge and take the laws into his own hand, or he must be subject to a government that will protect him. And for this purpose the government must have its police force. And if a Christian man may be a magistrate, a sheriff, or a constable or member of the city police, then he may be a sailor or a soldier, a commander in the fleet or army. There is nothing wrong in the one case more than the other. There is no more sin in being a commodore or general than there is in being a justice of the peace or the head of the government. The Rev. W. E. Boardman has briefly and very pointedly presented this idea in some foot-notes to his "Higher Christian Life." We would also refer those who desire to study the arguments on the justifiableness of war, as against Dr. Wayland and others of his school, who condemn all wars as useless, immoral and wicked, to the introductory chapter of Capt. H. W. Halleck's "Elements of Military Art and Science," and to the authors therein named. This work is a valuable one, combining the results of fine scholarship and of patient and extensive study. The introductory chapter, though short for the subject, is so exhaustive as to leave scarcely anything else to be said. We think his positions are ably and triumphantly sustained: but we need hardly add, we earnestly plead against war.

In the New Testament we read:

"And the soldiers likewise demanded of him, saying, And what shall we do? And he said unto them, Do violence to no man, neither accuse any falsely, and be content with your wages.'—*Luke* iii. 14. We do not know whether these soldiers were Jews or Romans, but the probability is, they were proselytes in the service of Herod Antipas, or of Philip, and in either case they were in the Roman service. The Greek term used here does not signify soldiers merely, but soldiers (*strateumenoi*) actually in arms, or under marching orders for battle. And as we learn from Josephus, that Herod was at this time engaged in war with Aretas, a king of Arabia, it is highly probable that Michaelis is right in saying that the military who came to John were a part of Herod's army, then marching from Galilee, and passing through the region where John was preaching. If this be correct, it is worthy of special notice, that John does not assume to decide between Herod and the Arabian king, nor say anything as to the lawfulness or justice of the war, but simply, and in his usual boldness and directness of style, tells the soldiers how to behave. In those days, armies were not as well provided for as they are now. They were not under the same discipline that our soldiers are as to private property. The custom was to make the country occupied by troops support them. And, consequently, the soldiers were strongly tempted to violence. And if they could not obtain such provisions and spoils as they wished from the inhabitants in any other way, they brought charges against them, falsely accusing them of disloyalty, rebellion, conspiracy, or some crime, by which they could justify themselves for taking by violence what they wanted. Hence the propriety of John's Knox-Latimer style of preaching to them. "Do violence to no man, neither accuse any falsely; and be content with your wages." As if he had said, Take nothing by unlawful means. Do not manufacture charges against the people. Accuse no one falsely. Be faithful, obedient, enduring. Find no fault with your service. Murmur not at your pay. Observe, then, John does not condemn their profession. He does not say, it was sinful for them to be soldiers, and that they must leave military service before they could please God. But he does tell them that they must not do any wrong thing under pretext that their calling required or excused it. Men in the army and the navy, as in all other professions, and everywhere, should be Christians.

The state of the question, then, is this; Most wars we think are wicked, unlawful and unjustifiable, either in the sight of God or man; but we do not believe that every war is sinful. Nor do we believe that the Gospel forbids the followers of Christ to engage in the military profession. We not only do not find any direct prohibition of war in the Bible, but on the contrary we have in the Old Testament "the wars of the Lord." We find God commanding war and conquest. And if all wars are unjustifiable and sinful, how is it that our Lord and his apostles have not expressly prohibited the military profession in the most unequivocal and positive terms? And, moreover, if every war is sinful, how is it we find so many pious men in the army? men as eminent for piety as for courage in the march, patience in the camp, and efficiency in the storm of battle? And the centurions whose history we are here studying are as commendable for their faith and extraordinary devotion as for their loyalty in the service of the pagan emperor of Rome. Our purpose here, however, is not to encourage war. We believe that most of the wars of our day are unnecessary and unjustifiable. And we believe the tendency of the Gospel is to do away with them from the earth; and that if all men were fully under its influence there would be no wars. Our purpose in the following pages, is mainly to show that it is not impossible for soldiers to be pious—that their condition is not in itself so sinful, that they are to be excused from a religious life, because they are soldiers or marines.

It is no doubt true that it is much harder for some men to be religious than others, just as it costs some men more to be decent than it would cost others to become saints. Some men are so constitutionally wicked—have so professionally and thoroughly devoted themselves to sin, that they are not only totally depraved, but their faculties are severally and alone, each by itself in need of an entire conversion for itself. But what then? Must we despair? By no means. JESUS CHRIST is the Saviour of sinners, even of the chief of sinners. And the more desperate the case, the more glory to the medical man that can heal it. Our great aim, then, in this volume, is to give an expository history of the Four Centurions, officers of the Roman army in Judea in apostolic times, who were to a greater or less degree brought under the power of the Gospel, or at least made acquainted with our Lord's history and doctrines; and to illustrate the fact, that eminent piety in a soldier is consistent with the loftiest courage—that in truth, the Church of God may and does exist in earthly armies. It is certainly very desirable that military men, officers and privates in the army, should be constantly reminded that there have been found in all ages in their profession, men whose piety, to say the least, would bear a comparison with that of any other profession. It is a necessary encouragement to them to know that men of their own class, men in every respect by birth and education and daily circumstances like themselves, have been truly pious. This should keep them from despairing. The cases we have tried to illustrate show, also, that God employs a great variety of means or instruments by which to bring men to a knowledge of saving truth; and that in some instances a high standard of piety has been displayed under great disadvantages. Men in the army and navy are accustomed to decision, promptness in action, and to meet with opposition and to endure discipline, to display a lofty courage and a devotion to their country and the cause they defend. It is perfectly consistent, therefore, that when it pleases God to reveal himself to them, they should show the same manful decision and courage in behalf of the Gospel.

I.

THE CENTURION OF CAPERNAUM.

AND when Jesus was entered into Capernaum, there came unto him a centurion, beseeching him, and saying, Lord, my servant lieth at home sick of the palsy, grievously tormented. And Jesus saith unto him, I will come and heal him. The centurion answered and said, Lord, I am not worthy that thou shouldest come under my roof: but speak the word only, and my servant shall be healed. For I am a man under authority, having soldiers under me; and I say to this *man*, Go, and he goeth; and to another, Come, and he cometh; and to my servant, Do this, and he doeth *it*. When Jesus heard *it*, he marvelled, and said to them that followed, Verily I say unto you, I have not found so great faith, no, not in Israel. And I say unto you, That many shall come from the east and west, and shall sit down with Abraham, and Isaac, and Jacob, in the kingdom of heaven: but the children of the kingdom shall be cast out into outer darkness: there shall be weeping and gnashing of teeth. And Jesus said unto the centurion, Go thy way; and as thou hast believed, *so* be it done unto thee. And his servant was healed in the self-same hour.—*Matthew* viii. 5-13. See also *Luke* vii. 1-10.

1.—*The Coming to Jesus.*

IT seems to us that this narrative is one of the most beautiful gems that so profusely adorn the Gospel history. It is the picture of a religious soul in a lovely and child-like form, revealing an extraordinary faith under great disadvantages.

And when Jesus was entered into Capernaum. The *time* of this miracle was shortly after our Lord came down from the mount where he had delivered his inimitable sermon, and not long after the miracle at the wedding in Cana of Galilee.

The *scene* of this miracle was the city of Capernaum, celebrated in the history of our Lord, though scarcely known in Old Testament times. Though born in Bethlehem of parents who belonged to Nazareth, our Lord made his own home chiefly at Capernaum. While in subjection to his parents—from early childhood till he was thirty years of age—he seems to have dwelt in Nazareth; but about the time that he commenced his public ministrations, or soon after his baptism, he "came and dwelt in Capernaum." This city was therefore the centre of his operations. To it we find him generally returning from his various itinerant missions. It was situate on the northwestern side of the lake of Gennesareth, called also the sea of Galilee. It was a Jewish city, at this time held by a Roman garrison in Herod's pay. There is still some doubt whether the precise spot on which it stood has been identified. *Ritter* and others suppose the *Tell Hum* of our day to mark its site; but our countryman, *Dr. Robinson*, and others, think *Kuhn Minyeh*, about three miles farther north, is its true site. However this may be, it is incontrovertible that our Lord's prediction concerning this city has been long since fulfilled. "Thou, Capernaum, which art exalted unto heaven, shalt be brought down to hell; for if the mighty works which have been done in thee, had been done in Sodom, it would have remained until this day. But I say unto you, that it shall be more tolerable for the land of Sodom in the day of judgment than for thee." *Matth.* xi. 23, 24.

Although this city was our Lord's home during the years of his public ministry, and notwithstanding He gave its inhabitants many evidences of his power to work miracles and to save, still they were remarkable for their infidelity, impenitence and general wickedness, and hence his denunciation of their sins for rejecting Him and continuing in their rebellion. Their abuse of great privileges augmented their guilt until their condemnation was greater than that of Sodom.

There came unto Him a centurion. Our word centurion is from the Latin *centum*, a hundred, and means literally a Roman officer commanding a hundred men, corresponding nearly to our captain. (See Adams' Rom. Antiq., p. 370.) The title centurion was, however, used with so much latitude, that it sometimes signified one who led a subdivision of a Roman legion, without fixing precisely its number. In the following places we find mention made of persons called centurions. Beside the passages referred to as texts above, *Matth.* xxvii. 54; *Acts* xi., xx., xxii., xiii., xxiv., xxvii., xxviii. The first convert to Christianity after the crucifixion from among the Gentiles whose name is known to us was Cornelius, a centurion of the Italian band at Cesarea, of whom we have more to say in another chapter. At least four centurions are favorably spoken of in the New Testament.

Some think the centurion of *Matthew* now before us the same who is called a nobleman of Capernaum in *John* iv., who came to Jesus, and begged mercy for his son. But there is no reason to suppose them the same. There are some striking points of resemblance, it is true, in the two narratives; but our Lord was never straitened for motives nor for means of showing his mercy. In both cases, the person asking help occupied a high position in society, and the person at the point of death was young, and the cure was wrought at a distance; and in both cases, the faith of the person making the application was remarkable; and our Lord was glorified by both miracles. Still there are points dissimilar—so dissimilar that the cases must be distinct. The one was a Jewish nobleman, looking for the Messiah; the other was a Roman officer, who had but little, if any, information concerning the great Hebrew that was so long and so ardently looked for as the Messiah. The Jewish nobleman makes application to Jesus in behalf of a son, who was nigh unto death with a fever; the Roman officer applies for aid for a servant (a slave), who was afflicted with paralysis. One miracle was wrought by our Lord when he was at Cana, the other when he was in the streets of Capernaum. But that which most distinguishes between the miracles was the faith of the applicants. The Jewish nobleman's faith was feeble. He besought our Lord that he would come and heal his son, for he was at the point of death. *John* iv. 27. He seems not to have thought that Jesus could heal his son, unless he visited him, and, like a medical man, on the spot should examine the patient, and prescribe according to the symptoms. Hence, we hear him saying, "Sir, come down ere my child die." But the centurion said, "Lord, I am not worthy that thou shouldest come under my roof: but speak the word only, and my servant shall be healed."

There is some difference of opinion among interpreters as to the identity of the cases recorded by *Matthew* and *Luke*. Cavillers have attempted to make out a contradiction between them. In regard to which, let it be remembered, we have no positive proof that both evangelists refer to the same case. It is not impossible but that there were two instances very much alike. Their circumstances may have been mainly coincident, and yet not identical. But on the supposition that we have two accounts of the same case, we find no difficulty in harmonizing them. They agree as to the characters, time and place, and substantially in the details. The only difference is that *Luke* is more particular in his chronology, and is more full, and gives us more details of outward events than are preserved in *Matthew*. *Luke* says the centurion sent the elders of the Jews, who besought Jesus to grant his request, saying that he was worthy, for he loveth our nation and hath built us a synagogue. But *Matthew*, in saying that the centurion came unto Jesus, does not contradict *Luke's* statement. He does not say that he had *not* sent his friends the elders of the Jews, nor does *Luke* say that he did not follow after them himself.

The probable state of the case was, that at first he sent, and being anxious, he followed afterward himself. And each of the evangelists records that part of the transaction which made the deepest impression on his mind, or seemed to him the most important. And as *Luke* was most familiar with Gentiles, and seems to have written his memoirs of our Lord especially for them, he records that this Roman officer was so kind to the Jews that their elders were his friends and interceded in his behalf, while *Matthew*, writing for his own countrymen, the Jews, was the most impressed with the fact that the centurion, a Roman officer, came himself to our Lord, who was a Jew. And besides, if this explanation is not sufficient, then we may adopt the legal maxim, and say— that which we do through or by another, is done by us. We may appear in court by our attorney or lawyer. We may be said to build a house, though we employ a carpenter to do it. A farmer may be said to plough and reap, although he employs laborers to do it for him. Such language is common, and obtains in all tongues. There is then no handle here for the enemies of the Gospel with which to work up a discrepancy between the evangelists. There is no contradiction between them; but on the contrary, by a candid and intelligent comparison of the two accounts, we obtain a more full history than we could get from either separately, and at the same time have an incidental or undesigned proof of their truthfulness as writers. Such minor variations are common in all written and oral narrations.

The elders sent to convey the centurion's message interceded for him, saying: "That he was worthy for whom he should do this, for he loveth our nation, and hath built us a synagogue."—*Luke* vii. 3–5.

A synagogue was a chapel or place of worship, where the Jews held their meetings for reading and expounding the holy Scriptures, but perhaps not common among them till after the captivity in Babylon. And as the centurion commanded the Roman garrison at Capernaum, he probably thought it would have a good effect upon the restless, turbulent Jews, who were so bitter in their prejudices against the Romans, if he showed them kindness. Soldiers and sailors are proverbially liberal with their means, and prompt to support public institutions. It was, however, a remarkable instance of good feeling, even if there was a measure of political expediency in it, for a Roman centurion out of his small salary to build a Hebrew synagogue.

We must not think, however, that we can purchase the grace of God by our charities. The centurion did not think of claiming the divine interposition because he had built a synagogue for the Jews. He did not speak of this at all. Nor is there any merit in religious duties to atone for our sins, or to give us a claim upon divine mercy on account of them. We should no doubt build houses of worship, and support the institutions of the Gospel, and we should read the Word of God, and hear his Gospel preached; but the means of grace are not to be substituted for Christ. The divine promise is that we shall find a blessing, if we seek, but not *because* we seek. The use of the means of grace is not the procuring cause of salvation, but the channel or way in which we are to find it. They bring Christ before us. It was when Lydia was in the synagogue on the Sabbath day that she heard Paul preach, and the Lord opened her heart to understand what she heard. It was when the Ethiopian was reading Isaiah, as he was returning from the worshipping of the Lord at Jerusalem, that the Spirit sent Philip to him to preach unto him Jesus. They were all found in the diligent, prayerful use of the means.

"Beseeching him and saying, Lord, my servant lieth at home, sick of the palsy, grievously tormented." *My servant*—literally "my boy"—a common and familiar term as *garçon* in French, or as we use the word *boy* for a favorite servant without regard to his age. *Luke* calls him a slave, and so interpreters generally understand the word *doulos*. *Calvin* suggests that he was a slave of rare fidelity and endowments, and hence the master's greater solicitude to save his life.

Lieth at home—literally is prostrate in the

house—*sick of the palsy.* It would seem that paralysis is not wholly a modern disease, as neuralgia or dyspepsia are said to be. Critically speaking, there may be some difference between palsy and paralysis, though the first term seems to be only a contraction of the latter; but in the New Testament they seem to be spoken of as quite the same thing, and as coming under our term apoplexy. The original here signifies a relaxation of the nerves of one side. The palsy prevailed in our Lord's day, and does still in the East. But there is scarcely any description in the New Testament of the diseases that prevailed in Judea in his day.

Grievously tormented—terribly, fearfully distressed—is in great agony and at the point of death, as in *Luke.* Now it is entirely a mistake, as some critics say, that in such a case of palsy there was no consciousness, no agony, no suffering. It may .be true that torment or agony does not always accompany the palsy. But there is a form of this disease that is attended by violent cramps and strong pains, and is exceedingly dangerous. Trench says the discase in this case was paralysis, with contraction of the limbs and joints, and was, therefore, a case of extreme suffering as well as of great danger. The Greek term for *grievously tormented* is from the name of a Lydian stone, upon which metals were proved, and hence it came to be used for applying an engine of torture in the examination of criminals, and metaphorically to afflict, torment. And hence here it is applied to a paralytic who is suffering violent pains.

II.

THE CENTURION OF CAPERNAUM CONTINUED

2.—The Peculiar Excellence of his Faith.

And Jesus saith unto him, I will come and heal him—that is, I will grant your request. I will save your servant. I am ready even to go to your house. Our Lord's reply then was prompt and gracious, marked with a confidence and dignity that showed that he was conscious of inherent power to work such a miracle as would save this servant. And now in the centurion's reply and our Lord's commendation of him we have an instance of extraordinary faith —of strong and discriminating faith—and of a miracle wrought without personal contact or immediate presence. Happily for us, this case will enable us to consider the nature of faith, which is an essential thing both in society and in religion. For such is our constitution that we cannot live without faith. We must have faith in ourselves and in one another, and in God and in his Word and works. It is by faith we know the history of the creation, and receive all our knowledge of past ages. We live by faith from day to day. We go to sleep at night confident of the coming morning, whether we live to see it or not. We have faith in the ordinances of heaven, and trust in the regularity of the laws which God has imposed upon nature. They are all his servants.

We trust in our *senses*, though they have often deceived us. We have faith in our *fellow men*, though they have often cruelly deceived us. A battle is fought and a kingdom is risked through faith in the intelligence of a spy. The merchant sends his vessel to the other side of the globe in charge of his captain, or ships a vast amount of goods to his correspondents, or buys thousands of dollars' worth of exchange, all on faith. The general must trust his officers and men, and they must have faith in him and in one another. And though some soldiers have turned traitors, and some clerks and consignees have been heartless villains, still, so essential is the principle of faith in society, that we must act on it. We cannot do without it. Without faith the affairs of society must stand still, and society itself is nothing but a mountain of sand. FAITH, then, is not a mere abstraction, nor the invention of cunning priests by which to put a yoke upon the people's necks to hold them down while they help themselves to their purses. Faith is not something merely bound up in the Confession and Thirty-nine Articles. Nor is it a new faculty of the mind made to priestly order by the Council of Nice, or by the Synod of Dort, or by the Westminster Assembly, or by the British Parliament. In general, faith is not a supernatural thing. It is a simple, familiar principle of every-day life. Intellectually and in a religious sense it is the same thing. It is belief, trust, confidence. But religiously, it is trust in God, belief in all God has said to us, because He says it, and confidence in his mercy through his well-beloved Son Jesus Christ. Such a faith is the gift of God. It is produced by his Spirit. It is "a saving grace whereby we receive and rest upon Jesus Christ alone for salvation, as he is offered to us in the Gospel." We may then see why it is that the Scriptures speak of faith as being so important, and tell us that without faith we cannot please God, nor be saved. And it is certainly remarkable that the two most extraordinary instances of faith recorded in the New Testament should have been found among the heathen, and not in the Hebrew Church—this centurion and the Syro-Phœnician woman in *Matthew* xv. And of her case, our Lord did not speak of her toil and travel, nor of her expense and perseverance, submission, patience, humility and maternal solicitude in coming to Him, but specifies her faith as most worthy of notice; so here it is not the benevolence, nor charities, nor rank, nor soldierly demeanor, nor humility and perseverance of the centurion that our Lord commends as most worthy of admiration, but his faith. "Verily I say unto you, I have not found so great faith, no, not in Israel."

In the *first place*, then, is there anything in the centurion's case that justifies our Lord's commendation? Even *he marvelled* at it. That is, was filled with wonder, admiration, astonishment, speaking after our manner, that so discriminating and strong a faith in him should be professed by a Roman officer. And the Holy Spirit has no doubt preserved this record of our Lord's admiration, to teach us that this man's faith is to be imitated as well as wondered at. It was wonderful that a man under such natural disadvantages as had encompassed this pagan and soldier in his education and youth, and profession in manhood, should recognize what the Jewish rulers failed to see, and should profess a greater faith than any of their race—a race heroic by faith—had ever before displayed.

First. It was to be marvelled at that such faith was found *outside* of the Hebrew Church. The term *faith* used in the text does not of itself necessarily imply saving views of Christ as a Redeemer; but from its connection, we think it proper so to consider it. Primarily it means here confidence in Jesus as having power to heal without personal contact. *But speak the word only,* said he, *and my servant shall be healed.* *Wetstein* and some others understand this to mean: "Command by a word and my servant shall be healed." This was certainly an extraordinary profession of faith for a man to make in a Hebrew, who had not himself been brought up in the creed and catechism of Abraham. *No, not in Israel*—that is, not among the chosen people. Not one of the disciples or apostles, even, had as yet made such a profession of faith in him. They had the prophets and Moses, whose writings clearly pointed out the work and character of the Messiah, yet they had not professed such faith in him. *Not in Israel* is emphatic. Israel was the memorial name of Jacob for his having prevailed with God so as to become a prince, and from him all Jews prefer to be called Israelites, just as the people of Rome assumed to be called Romans in honor of *Romulus.* The meaning then is: I have not found such an instance of faith among the Jews, who are distinguished for their princes, who have prevailed with God on account of their faith. They have had men of heroic faith, but not such an instance as this.

The distinguishing excellence of the centurion's faith, then, did not consist in his having an exalted idea of God, and believing that he was the Creator and governor of all things. *David* had as great faith in the works of creation and Providence as he had, and no doubt knew a great deal more than he did. And *Cicero* and many of the heathen had some grand ideas of the Divine power. He could say: "Nihil est quod Deus efficere non posset, et quidem sine labore ullo," etc. (*De Nat. D., lib.* 3.)

Nor did the peculiar excellence of the centurion's faith lie in his belief in miracles. All Jews, and even all the heathen, believed in miracles. It was a part of the common faith of the whole world, and is so still, with exceptions as rare as idiots. The peculiarity, the distinguishing excellence, then, of this man's faith consisted in this—that he, being a Gentile and a Roman officer, accustomed to see men having influence and authority regarded with great ceremony, should believe that Jesus, who was outwardly a mere man—a Hebrew—in humble circumstances, and without any of the pomp or signs of power that he was accustomed to recognize, wielded the heavenly powers, and had as complete a control over them, and over all diseases and spirits as he had over his servants and soldiers.

Second. It was worthy of special attention that such faith was found in *a soldier.* Our Lord was at this time surrounded by the Scribes, and probably in the house of a Pharisee, but it was in the Roman soldier that he found the greatest faith. As the profession of arms is not in itself sinful—is not a sin *per se*—so neither is the term soldier synonymous with cruelty or bloodthirstiness, nor with drinking, debauchery and lawlessness. If there are butchers among soldiers like *Nana Sahib,* there are also *Havelocks* who are as distinguished for refinement and kindness of feeling as for lofty courage. We regard war as a terrible thing, but it is sometimes the less of two evils. War is better than national disgrace, or such loss of national honor and position as should destroy our self-respect and happiness. Gladly would we have our cannon turned into church bells, and our shot and balls into railroads, and our men of war into merchant ships, if it were expedient. But it is not, nor will it be, until men shall learn war no more. Such is the depravity of mankind that one sword is necessary to keep another in its scabbard. It is not necessary here, however, to enter upon the question about the lawfulness of war in Christian states. The only point here insisted on is, that because a man is a soldier, he is not of necessity the greatest of sinners. A man is under no necessity to serve Satan, because he serves the government as a soldier. The army is not a favorable school for piety. The military profession presents occasions and temptations to idleness and manifold wrong-doing. It is an excited, spasmodic, irregular kind of life. The soldier and the sailor are often without Sabbaths and sanctuaries, and under peculiar temptations to forget God, yet it has pleased God that his grace should have many heroes even in armies and camps and naval ships. If the military profession was a sin *per se*, then, instead of having chaplains to preach the Gospel and administer the sacraments of the Church in our army and navy, they should urge the men to desertion. But when the soldiers crowded to hear John the Baptist preach, as well as the Scribes and Pharisees, did he tell them to desert, and join a Peace society? No; but he did tell them to do no violence and to be content with their wages, and not to accuse any man falsely. Soldiers are found also listening to the words of truth as they fell from the lips of the Great Teacher himself. But he did not tell them to leave their profession because it was a sin. In the New Testament we have *four different centurions* brought under the power of the Gospel. The one before us owed allegiance to a heathen emperor, yet he possessed greater faith than any in Israel. And what shall we say of Abraham, Moses, Joshua and David—men of preëminent faith, and yet heroes in battle? And what shall we say of Captain Page, Captain Gordon, Colonel Gardiner, General Burns and General Sir Henry Havelock, and many others in our times?

III.

CENTURION OF CAPERNAUM CONTINUED.

3.—Evidences of the Centurion's Faith.

In the *next place*, then, let us look at *the proofs or evidences of the centurion's faith*. And here observe, *First*. His tender care for his servant. But could not a Roman officer be kind to his servants and faithful to his soldiers, without having any knowledge of the true religion? Do not the heathen practise many virtues? We answer, certainly they do. There are some actions recorded of heathens that are worthy of imitation. But admitting that there are some few things lovely and excellent among Pagan nations, we do not by any means admit that their ethics are to be compared with those of Christianity, or that they are not in need of the Gospel. By no means. The picture drawn of them by the apostle in his epistles is still true. Nor do we allow that the admission of any good thing to heathendom is antagonistic to the Gospel. The morals of heathendom, even if they were a hundred times better than they are, do not contradict nor supersede Christianity. The teachings of tradition, the light of nature, and of conscience and God's Spirit are the teachers of all men, and are quite sufficient to account for the glimpses or guesses at truth that we find among the heathen. Considering the physical and moral unity of all human races, it would be strange if there had not been found in heathendom an unconscious prophesying that proves the necessity of a Saviour, just as their sacrifices prove a conscious need for some atonement for sin. Indeed it would be strange if there were not some fragmentary truths in all nations and in all ages, resembling one another, and altogether bearing testimony to God's own original copy and to the complete edition of his own revealed truth.

Second. The *completeness of this Roman soldier's character*, as seen in the care of his servant as well as in his public spirit, deserves special notice. His attention to the religious wants of the people around him, nurtured his humane feelings for his own household. His charity did not all go abroad. He did not make his generosity toward the Jews an excuse for neglecting home duties. His public regard for the Hebrews was not made a veil to cover up selfishness. And as a historic fact, it is to be observed, that true religion is always found developing what is lovely and of good report, noble, kind and reasonable. This centurion's anxiety for the recovery of his slave is, however, the more remarkable when we consider that he was a Roman, and the age in which he lived. His conduct is a remarkable contrast with that of the eloquent Cicero, who thought it necessary to excuse himself for having had some feeling at the death of one of his household. Ordinarily in that age and among the Romans, slaves were denied the sympathy that belonged to other human beings.

In whatever way we may account for the morality and tenderness of this Roman officer toward his servant, we find them in connection with, colored by, and developed in an extraordinary faith. His benevolence and charity, if not called into being by his religious faith, were certainly ennobled and made more delicate by it. It is indeed true that morality is not piety, but there is no consistent or true piety without good morals. It is true, that high social affections, amiable instincts, commercial virtues—promptness in business, capacity for business, and integrity on 'Change, are not to be substituted for penitence and faith in Christ, yet they are in every way commendable. But the instinct of kindness toward a servant or dependent may in itself be no more in a religious way than instinct tenderness toward a horse or dog. And does not this instinct tenderness for animals exist among the heathen who have never heard of the name of Jesus? May not a *deist*, who does not believe in the Bible, bind a poultice to his wounded hound, or an *atheist*, who denies immortality, and says there is no God, weep over the groans of his dying steed? May it not be, then, that a man is sober, intelligent, and industrious—that he has been a dutiful son, and is a faithful husband, an indulgent father, a kind neighbor, a good citizen, an upright and honest man, and that still he is not a Christian? If he is all this, let us thank God for it; but let us remember that one thing he lacks yet, and that one thing is love to God—a supreme regard for his will—an habitual reference of all to his law as the standard of right and wrong—an habitual trust in God as a sinner reconciled to Him through Jesus Christ. Now is it not fairly a matter within your own experience or observation, that a man may have amiable instincts and social and business virtues, and yet not have the fear of God before his eyes? There is want of spirituality spread over all he is and does. There is no spirit of prayer, of love to God, nor panting after holiness, nor habitual striving to please God. Is it not true that a lady may be found weeping at the theatre over a tragedy, who has never wept over her guilt as a sinner, for rejecting Christ; or in ecstasy at an opera, who has never rejoiced in the love of God shed abroad in her heart by the Holy Ghost? A taste for poetry and the fine arts does not always imply a love of holiness. Nor does a reformation of manners always imply regeneration, though regeneration is seen only by a reformation of life. Every conversion to God yields the fruits of true obedience to his laws. Salvation by grace does not lead to licentiousness, nor does justification by faith excuse us from good works, but the rather impels us to them, so that those who believe in justification by faith, and in salvation by sovereign grace, are of all men the hardest and most persevering workers. They work diligently because God works in them, and they believe God is helping them. It is not true, then, that Christianity diminishes in any measure a man's tenderness for his fellow men; nor does it make a man any the less trustworthy as a mechanic, merchant or soldier. On one occasion the general in command of the English army in India was told that the insurgents were about making an attack on one of his positions, and he ordered out a certain regiment to oppose them; but his aid replied, that regiment could not go, for "they were all drunk." "Then," said the commander, "call out Havelock's *saints;* they are never drunk, and Havelock is always ready." Accordingly the bugle sounded—the ranks of the "saints" closed sternly up, and with him at their head, who had so often led them in prayer, the troops charged on the enemy and scattered them in flight.* This true history is its own interpreter. For the soldiers who were so sober and so much given to singing psalms, reading the Bible, and prayer, that they were called *Havelock's saints*, because he had so taught them, were the very men of all others to meet the enemy. And never did they fail to perform their duty faithfully to their general, their country and their God. The history of war from the beginning till now, does not present a record of greater courage or of more lofty heroism in battle, than we find in Havelock's Indian campaigns with his Highlanders and the 13th Infantry.

* Headley's Life of Havelock, p. 48.

It is not then true, that the Gospel builds up the Church on the ruins of civilization. Christianity wages no war against the fine arts, nor does it preach any crusade against the elegant accomplishments or proprieties of society. Going to church is not to make people vinegar-faced; nor is true enlightened piety a lowering gloom, nor a moping melancholy. A man does not cease to be a gentleman by becoming a Christian. On the contrary, he is only half, and the least half of a gentleman before, for until he is a Christian, even if he is all that a gentleman should be toward his fellow men, he has not done his duty to his God, and is therefore sadly wanting in that *completeness*—that high finish of character that constitutes the highest style of a gentleman—*a thoroughly honest man* both toward his fellow men and God. And shall we not imitate this Roman officer in his tenderness toward his servant? Among the great evils of our times are the insubordination of domestics, the precocity of children, and the selfishness of masters and the heads of establishments. Flunkies affect to be lords, and "the queens of society" are in the kitchen. So feelingly and so universally is the remark made, that "servants are the greatest plagues of life," that we are almost ready to wish our times were thrown back to the feudal ages, when, if there was a distinction in rank, there was also some care for subordinates, and some household pride and affection. But now household relations are transient, spasmodic, uncertain—a mere convenience or necessity for dollars and cents. The social and religious improvement of the one part, and the promoting of the welfare of the other part, are respectively overlooked. Nor is it easy to see where the remedy lies. We can, however, look back to former years, and sigh that in this particular the past is better than the present. The evils of society, as it now exists among us, are very serious, both as it regards the well-being of its members in this world, and the spiritual necessities of both masters and servants, heads of establishments and the young under their care. It is perfectly obvious that we are tending in our day to anarchy and lawlessness, and to a system of pauperism, which only the strongest governments of Europe are able to bear. And the root of this evil is the neglect of home education, the want of family government, instruction and religion.

Third. Another evidence of this centurion's faith is seen in his remarkable humility. His address to our Lord, saying, *I am not worthy that thou shouldest come under my roof*, is the more remarkable when we consider the relative position of the parties. Jesus was a Jew—belonged to a people despised by the Romans. There was no earthly pomp or greatness about him. But here we see an officer of the Roman army commanding in a conquered province, whose master was the conqueror of the world—rich, influential and powerful—so struck with the dignity and moral excellence of Jesus, that, wholly regardless of the disparity of their rank, he openly professed himself unworthy to receive a personal visit from him. Indeed, so remarkable was his humility, that if our Lord had not commended his faith, we should have been at a loss which to admire the most. Indeed, they were inseparable, and are so still. The root of his humility was his faith. The excellence of condescension is that it proceeds from true greatness. His humility is seen in his declaration of unworthiness, as well in sending the Jewish elders as in his declaration about our Lord's coming to his house. "Wherefore neither thought I myself worthy to come unto thee." "Lord, trouble not thyself: for I am not worthy that thou shouldest enter under my roof." *Luke* vii. 6, 7. How vastly different this from the style of the Pharisees. The Gentile soldier was a better Christian than the Hebrew elders. So great was his humility that he did not consider himself good enough, nor of sufficient value to have the honor of our Lord's personal presence at his quarters.

But it deserves to be remembered that such humility as this is found only in connection with true faith. Without reverence there is no piety. The Roman soldier was not given to stereotyped and vain phrases. He was not quick to make vain professions. But in a few words declared what he felt. "Speak the word only, and my servant shall be healed." Short, explicit, and full of meaning, just such words as such a military man would be likely to use. He knew nothing about the lore of the schools. He had no catechetical definition of faith on hand. He had never read a theological treatise, hence he made his profession of faith in the language that his profession suggested. And as faith is the same thing, whether found in a heathen, a Jew or a Christian, whether found in the heart of a soldier, a sailor, a merchant, or of a philosopher, so there is no mistake as to his meaning. The forms and modes of expressing our faith may be greatly diversified; but faith itself is the same thing. Hence he, referring to his own experience and to his own official power, said: "I say to one, Go, and he goeth; and to another, Come, and he cometh; and to my servant, Do this, and he doeth it;" so says he, I believe you have the will and the power to heal my servant. "Speak the world only, and my servant shall be healed." This is a most lively, laconic picture of Roman authority, brevity of command and promptitude of obedience.

Now as faith is trust in God, so it is altogether a different thing from the haughty and ignorant spirit of self-conceit, which is sometimes called independence or manliness. Now, if by being independent, a young man means that he will earn his own living by honest toil and owe no man anything—that he will rise in the world by his own exertions and not owe it to the patronage of others—that he will be honored by his own labors rather than by those of his father and mother, then we bid him God speed. This may all be quite right. But if by independence, he means that he will be bound by no ties to other human beings—that he will owe no allegiance to any will but his own, and live within and by himself—then we say, he is quite at fault. He is trying to do what is wholly impracticable. He will never be able to pay his God, his parents and his country what he owes them. Nor can he live alone. Without a friend the world is a desert. Without something to love and confide in, man is a miserable creature. This morbid, affected love of independence that throws off the obligations of society—that frees a man from the moral principles taught him by his parents because they are old-fashioned, and affects to make a man his own lord and master, is *revolutionary* in politics, *atheistic* in religion, and a monstrous deformity. And it proves jealousy and littleness on the part of him that indulges it, rather than true manliness of character.

Do not err, however, as to the centurion's *humility*. He was not blindly pinning his faith to anybody's sleeves, nor was he impaling his heart for daws to peck at. He was not *fawning on* the Emperor of Rome, nor *flattering* the commanding general of the Roman legions, nor *telling* lies, nor offering bribes to the Governor of Cesarea, nor electioneering for a nomination to high places and emoluments. His homage was voluntary, and proceeded from his own conviction. He came to Jesus of Nazareth to save his dying servant. And according to the divine promise, having humbled himself, he was exalted. He did not think himself worthy that Jesus should enter his house, but our Lord entered his heart. His humility was before honor. It was just the reverse with the Pharisee—he considered Jesus unworthy to be in his house, or that he was doing him a great honor to invite him to his house, and our Lord did not enter into his heart.

Fourth. It is in evidence as a proof of the centurion's extraordinary faith, that he did not require any assistance from the senses. His confidence was implicit, perfect in the presence and power of a will, which was itself not visible. Is it not remarkable that he did not desire Jesus to go with him—that he did not consider his *bodily* presence necessary for working the miracle? He did not consider any personal contact necessary. He looked for the desired result not by any ordinary treatment, much less by any trickery. His faith was in the power of the Supreme Being, whose agent he believed Jesus to be, if he was not the very God of God himself, manifest in a human form. It is well known that even the heathen had some idea of the God of the Jews, and of angels and spirits, and had some notion of God's assuming human forms, and coming among men. Homer is full of this. The centurion in command at the crucifixion had some confused idea of Divinity on earth; or that the Son of God could suffer as a man on the cross. I am satisfied that the ordinary method of explaining the faith of this centurion and of Cornelius the centurion of Cesarea, by considering them proselytes to Judaism, is not correct. It is not affirmed in either case, nor fairly implied. Indeed the very reverse seems to be implied in the terms used to express their piety, and by the contrast with Israel, in the history now under consideration. It is, however, true, that though brought up in the creed of Paganism, still he had of late years, by his residence in a Jewish town, sufficient opportunities to become familiar with Hebrew opinions and somewhat acquainted with the fame of Jesus. The miracles and history of the former ages of the Jewish nation were no doubt substantially known to him and believed in by him. Nor would this imply at all that he was a proselyte of the gate; but only that he was no longer a gross idolater, and had respect for the Hebrew faith and people. It is not easy to define how much, and just what kind of faith the centurion had before he came to Jesus; but we are sure, from the result, that he did right in applying to Jesus, and that he had faith enough to save his servant, and we hope faith enough to save his soul.

Fifth. The centurion's case is also the more remarkable, on account of the national prejudices that existed toward the Jews in the minds of all other nations, and which were returned with compound interest by the Jews toward all other people. The prejudices of race and religion were exceedingly strong between the Romans and the Jews, and at this time, their political subjection made the Jews more bitter than usual. The proud Roman usually felt contempt for the conquered Jew. But this centurion betrays no such feeling; nor does he assume any patronizing air on account of his military command, nor for what he has done for the Jews, nor does he resent the peculiar claims of the Hebrew religion. Taking the whole history into review, we cannot but hope that this centurion was truly converted to God. He could not have been ignorant of the main doctrines of the Hebrew religion. He must have known that they believed in one only living and true God, and that they claimed peculiar privileges as the people of God descended from Abraham; and as we find him here acknowledging himself unworthy of the personal regards of a Jew, and yet possessed of an unwavering faith that he could exercise as unquestioned power over diseases, as he himself could over his soldiers; and the more so, because this sense of unworthiness and this deep humility imply a sense of sin that could be produced only by the Holy Spirit. When, therefore, we put together his consciousness of sin—his feeling of unworthiness, and his high opinion of Jesus, and remember that his education as a Roman officer had been completed by gaining considerable knowledge of the world, and especially some knowledge of the Hebrews and of the religion of the God of Abraham, Isaac and Jacob—we conclude that the sickness of a favorite servant was overruled by a gracious sovereignty, so as to be made the occasion of his coming into direct contact with the Son of God, and of bringing out this confession of faith in Him.

Sixth. The form of his profession of faith proves its strength. "For I am," says he, "a man under authority, having soldiers under me: and I say to this man, Go, and he goeth; and to another, Come, and he cometh; and to my servant, Do this, and he doeth it." Therefore, says he, "speak the word only, and my servant shall be healed." This was emphatically a military profession. It was logical, simple, brief and straight out. His argument was *a fortiori*—from the weak to the stronger—from the less to the greater. He institutes a comparison between his military authority over his soldiers and servants and the power of Jesus over all things, or at least over spirits and diseases; and he says, I believe that you have all the powers of the invisible world under your command as fully as I have command over my soldiers. And even more than this seems implied. It is as if he had said, I, who am but a subordinate officer, issue my orders and they are promptly obeyed, although I am myself under the authority of my superiors, whom I implicitly obey; then much more have you the power to make diseases go or come at your simple word. I am an humble officer, and have command over only a few soldiers and servants, but thou art in command of the armies of heaven, and all things are obedient to thee. His belief that Jesus could heal at a distance implies his idea that our Lord possessed omniscience and omnipresence.

IV.

THE CENTURION OF CAPERNAUM CONTINUED.

4.—*This Roman officer still preaching the Gospel.*

First. Here is an incidental illustration of the *perfect humanity* of our Lord. "When Jesus heard it, he marvelled"—*wondered*, or more literally, was astonished, spoken in reference to his humanity. Our Lord's estate of humiliation was as real as his estate of exaltation. His body and soul were as truly human, as his Divinity was truly that of the Godhead. His human nature was perfect, and in it he was capable of grief, anger, wonder, or joy. The only difficulty here is "the mystery of godliness: God manifest in the flesh." The meaning of our Lord's marvelling, then, is not that he did not know the state of the centurion's mind before he spoke. He was as well acquainted with the nature of his faith, and the grounds upon which it rested, before the centurion had professed and explained it as he was afterward. The term used here also embraces the idea of admiration—such as is felt for the greatness and beauty of a thing. Our Lord then designed to express his admiration for the centurion's faith as extraordinary in this—that though nurtured in heathenism, yet his faith was superior to any he had met with among the children of Abraham. And this admiration the evangelist has expressed in natural language.

Second. We should learn from this history not to indulge in general and indiscriminate reflections upon whole communities and professions. We must not condemn men as classes. In the soldier's or sailor's life, in camps and fleets, there are many drawbacks to a Christian life; but where sin reigns, grace has abounded, and even reigned more gloriously. The profession of arms is not without its army of saints, confessors and martyrs, who have waged successful war with other than carnal weapons.

And if some lawyers have given occasion for calling their offices "dens of thieves," it does not follow that none of them are honest. If some merchants have sworn to false invoices, and sold goods inferior to their samples, it does not follow that they are all guilty of fraud. And if some officers of the army and navy do so far forget themselves as to swear as if they were with the army in Flanders, it does not prove that all soldiers must take the name of God in vain, nor that it is necessary to swear profanely in order to maintain authority over sailors and soldiers. Havelock did not swear at his men. But he did often pray and sing psalms with them, read the Bible to them, and teach them about Jesus Christ.

A most striking instance of this is recorded by the Rev. Mr. Brock, in his Life of Havelock, in his first campaign. The English army had just taken Rangoon, in which there is "a famous heathen temple devoted to the service of Boodh, which is known as the magnificent Shivey Dagoon Pagoda. It is deemed the glory of the city. Of a chamber of this building,

Havelock obtained possession for his own purposes. All around the chamber were smaller images of Boodh, in the usual position, sitting with their legs gathered up and crossed, and the hands resting on the lap in symbol and expression of repose. No great changes were necessary to prepare the place for Christian service. It needed no ceremonial exorcising to make it fit either for psalmody or prayer. Abominable idolatries had been witnessed there beyond all doubt, but no sacerdotal purifications were requisite ere adoration of the true God could be offered and service well-pleasing to Him, through Jesus Christ. Havelock remembered well that 'neither in this mountain nor yet at Jerusalem' were men to worship the Father now. To the true worshippers any place might become a place for worship. Even the pagoda of Shivey Dagoon might be none other than the house of God and the gate of heaven.

"Accordingly, it was announced that that would be the place of meeting. An officer relates that as he was wandering round about the pagoda on one occasion, he heard the sound, strange enough as he thought, of singing. He listened, and found that it was certainly psalm singing. He determined to follow the sound to its source, and started for the purpose. At length he reached the chamber, and what should meet his eye but Havelock, with his Bible and hymn-book before him, and more than a hundred men seated around him, giving earnest heed to his proclamation to them of the glad tidings of great joy. How had they got their light by which to read, for the place was in dark shade? They had obtained lamps for the purpose, and putting them in order, had lit them and placed them one by one in an idol's lap. There they were, those dumb but significant lamp-bearers, in constant use; and there they were, we may be well assured, to suggest stirring thoughts to the lieutenant and his men."

Here is a subject worthy of a painter. The city of Rangoon and its glory; a young British officer in a heathen temple with his Bible and hymn-book before him, and more than a hundred men seated around him, listening to the glad tidings of the Gospel, and the lamps that gave them light shining out of the laps and skulls of idols. Troops just led through the fury and smoke of battle, here assembled for prayer and singing psalms. This was an extraordinary sight. But it did not disqualify either the men or their commanding officer for the hardships and perils of war. The voice of Havelock, so often heard in prayer to the throne of grace in time of need, and in thanksgiving after great deliverances, was strong and steady in battle. When complaint was made to the Governor-General of India against Havelock, that he was "a pietist," "a ranting Methodist" or "a fanatic Baptist," and that he did nothing but pray with his men and teach them to sing psalms, and that his highest aim was to *baptize* them, Lord Bentick having examined into the subject, dismissed the complaint, saying, he wished Havelock "had baptized the whole army," for that, after a rigid examination of the official records, he found that Havelock's saints were the most sober, obedient and best behaved men in the regiment—"in short, the model soldiers of the army"—"and that wherever hard fighting was to be done, Havelock's saints were relied upon." Certainly, no commander ever had the confidence and obedience of his men more fully than he had. He was remarkable for the accuracy of his drill and the rigidness of his discipline. No other troops on earth have shown more coolness and precision under the rattling hail of musketry, nor amid the murdering crash of artillery, nor have any soldiers on earth surpassed Havelock's in the bayonet charge. Nor have we any knowledge of braver men in action than Vicars and Hammond before Sebastopol, and Lawrence and Havelock at Cawnpore and Lucknow, and yet these men were distinguished as men of prayer.

Some professions are, indeed, more favorable to a religious life than others; and yet it is in these unfavorable ones some of the brightest examples of the power of true godliness are found. There the reigning of grace over abounding sin has made it preëminent. The more temptations men have to resist, the more evil propensities they have to subdue, the more difficulties they have to struggle with, the more is their success to be commended. The more terrible the conflict, the brighter the victor's crown. Although the reputation of Nazareth was proverbially bad, yet out of it came the world's Redeemer. Shall we not, then, be cautious in judging of professions and classes, and not let our prejudices or passions lead us to erroneous, hasty, uncharitable judgments?

There are many more good and truly pious people in the world than we generally suppose. And there are a great many people that we should love, if we only knew them better. All men are not reprobates because some are. Judas was one of the twelve, yet the rest were true men. Peter loved his Lord, though he did once deny him, and is now no doubt a saint in heaven, whether he ever was a Pope in Rome or not—perhaps all the better saint, because he was not. Arnold's treachery does not prove that Washington did not love and serve his country till his death. What, then, if some church members are rude, unpolished, or even starched hypocrites, it does not follow that Christianity is not the true religion. We cannot have a community fit to live in until the practice of wholesale slandering, and cruel, rash, unfounded judgments are corrected. Public sentiment must be elevated and purified from the vulture-seeking of a neighbor's wrong-doings, and by speaking only the truth, and the truth only when necessary.

Third. Let us learn then to be more *charitable.* God is no respecter of persons, but whosoever feareth Him and worketh righteousness is accepted of Him. Salvation is indeed of the Jews, but not to be confined to them. It was with them as a reservoir until the fulness of time for causing it to flow forth to all the world. We rejoice that ours is not the only true Church—that we have no patent for ours as the only way to heaven. "Many," says our Lord, "shall come from the east and the west, and shall sit down with Abraham, and Isaac, and Jacob in the kingdom of heaven."

The centurion being a Roman—a Gentile —

such as the Jews considered altogetner excluded from the privileges of Messiah's kingdom, our Lord took the occasion to declare the sovereign grace of God toward the Gentiles, and to teach the Jews that their prejudices were wrong, for that all parts, even the remotest quarters of the earth, should receive the Gospel, and all nations flow into the kingdom of God. And that *the children of the kingdom,* that is, the Jews who claimed to have a peculiar and exclusive right to the privileges and blessings of Messiah's kingdom, because they were Abraham's descendants, *shall be cast out into outer darkness: there shall be weeping and gnashing of teeth.* "Outer darkness and weeping and gnashing of teeth" are a fearful image of the wretchedness and woe of those who fail to enter the kingdom of God. It is founded upon the banquet-chamber of the preceding verses, illuminated and filled with joyous guests; but outside, in the cold and cheerless dark, where is nothing but weeping and wailing and gnashing in rage and spite, are those that considered themselves the favorites of

God, and sure of heaven, because of their descent from the patriarchs. Oh, how dreadful to be an outcast from God's kingdom! How awful will be the disappointments of the day of judgment!

Fourth. The proofs of the reality of this miracle are easily apprehended. No collusion was possible. The household, the Jewish rulers and the public are all acquainted with the facts, and all admit the main points, namely: the centurion's servant is very ill—in the very agony of death—and the centurion coming to Jesus besought him to speak the word only and his servant shall be healed. And Jesus neither goes to his house nor touches nor sees the dying servant, but speaks the word and he is healed. Multitudes hear and know and admit that all this was true. And the common belief of all the people at that time in Capernaum is embodied in the simple and plain narrative of our evangelists. Christianity then is true. Jesus Christ is the Son of God, and the Almighty Saviour of all who believe in Him.

Fifth. Learn that disadvantages are not insuperable. Great difficulties in our way may be overcome. Not only is to bear, to conquer our fate; but to a heroic soul in the path of duty, "Danger's self is lure alone." And the greater the difficulties overcome in coming to Jesus, the greater our faith. The early disadvantages of the centurion resulted in giving superiority to his faith. His want of education in the knowledge of the true religion in his youth, and the unfavorable influences of his profession, made his faith all the more distinctive. The proudest triumphs of art, science, government and arms have been achieved by men who have reached success not from aristocratic loins, nor by royal road, but by overcoming almost insuperable difficulties. The men who rule us from their urns, and who had, while living, the greatest influence upon mankind, *were self-made men*—men who have pursued knowledge, truth and godliness under difficulties—who have risen superior to great disadvantages—who have carved their way to fame and fortune with their own hands.

We must strive to enter in, if we would be saved.

Sixth. In our Lord's commendation of the centurion, we see that it is according to the degree of a man's faith, that he is to be estimated. As if he had said he is the strongest man who has the most faith, for faith takes hold of omnipotence. The words, *Verily, I say unto you,* are intended to mark the commendation of the centurion's faith as something special. His faith was stronger than that of the nobleman who had come to Jesus for his dying child. We read of others who applied, saying: "*If* thou canst do anything, have compassion on us and help us." And the sisters of Bethany said, "Lord, *if* thou hadst been here, my brother had not died." And the father of the demoniac in agony and in uncertainty, cried out: "I believe, help thou my unbelief." But none of them said, *Speak the word only,* and the work of mercy is done. Martha and Mary seem, like the nobleman, to have thought our Lord's bodily presence necessary to heal. But the centurion has no *if,* nor idea of space in his faith, and hence our Lord's commendation was unqualified. His faith was unparalleled in Christ's power to heal at a distance, and without any personal contact.

Seventh. As the centurion's mind naturally run in the channel of his profession, and as in casting about for expressions or terms in which to declare his faith in Jesus, we find him building his faith upon the elements which his profession readily furnished, and declaring his faith by the forms of speech which his own mode of life suggested; so we should learn from his case, that God accepts our faith and our profession of our trust in him even when it is drawn out in the form of our calling or mode of life. The rules of military science among the Romans gave form to his profession of faith.* He felt and believed in the presence and power of the Roman emperor, though his person was not in Capernaum. As an officer in the army, he was under a present will, though no bodily form was present; and so

---

* "Sed hanc exceptionem concoquit sapientia fidelis ex ruditate militari pulchre elucens."—BENGEL.

he believed that Jesus could heal without personal contact. Nor is this the only instance. The heavens are always telling the glory of God. The daisy and the dewdrop declare the presence of God as well as the mightiest planet in the highest heavens. Nor is there any trade, calling or profession that is according to the laws of God, that may not in its way educate our soul for God and immortality, while it enables us to gain an honest living in the body. Perhaps we may illustrate this from the case of the shepherds and of the wise men of the East. Shepherds, like sailors, are close observers of the weather, winds and skies. They are proverbially superstitious, as people also usually are who dwell much alone among the mountains. To them the sighing of the storm, the moaning of the night winds, the clouds wreathing themselves around the headlands, or rolling up in columns, and marching off in unequalled grandeur over the mountains —all seem to be instinct with more than mortal life. It was natural, therefore, if such an expression may be used, where all was *super-*

natural, that the voice of angels should come to the shepherds on the winds from the melodies of the skies: "A multitude of the heavenly hosts praising God, and saying, glory to God in the highest, and on earth peace, good will toward men." They heard the glad tidings of a Saviour born, while watching their flocks by night on the Bethlehem plains—while engaged in their humble, honest occupation. And so of the Magi. In the clear starlit skies of the East, where one seems almost to see through the cerulean vaults to the eternal throne, the wise men were engaged in their profession, which was the study of the heavenly hosts, and while engaged in this study, a *star* is sent to guide them to the infant Redeemer. And so should it be with all our pursuits, whereby we make a living, and are brought into contact with the laws of God. The man that spades up the ground and sows the seed, and he who converts the solid rock into lime, and he who builds the brick with mortar into a solid wall; and the sunburnt sickle-man, and the hard-handed miner, who grinds the gold from the quartz, or attracts it from the sandy mass, no less than the electrician and astronomer, are all working with and by the laws of the Creator. The ladder by which Newton climbed from his apple-tree to the outposts of the universe was made by the laws of God. The Almighty went before him and laid his hand upon all space and matter, or the philosopher could never have climbed to the limits of our system. And shall we not adore the wisdom, the goodness, and the sovereign grace of God, that makes a man's business for him—so that it is a school for him, both for this life as well as for the life to come? Our calling or pursuit in life should be according to the will of God, and then our diligence in business, as well as our fervency in spirit, will be a means of grace—in both we shall serve the Lord. It is intended to educate us for heaven as well as gain for us a living upon earth. It is possible for us to make the best of both worlds. The Roman soldier read through the regulations of the art of war a *personal will*, and he knew that his authority extended in like manner to those that were placed under him; and in the unity and harmony, variety and yet concentration, movement, strategy, logistics and tactics of an army, he saw clearly the presence of an all-controlling, designing, supreme mind. And all this process he transferred to Jesus, and made all the invisible world as subordinate to him, as the inferiors of an army are to the commanding officer.

Wonderful is the condescension of our Maker! We are indeed poor, feeble creatures. We are almost invisible particles in the vast universe, yet each one of us is so bound up with other atoms in the divine volume of Divine benevolence and omnipotence, that not one of us is forgotten before God. The hairs of our head are numbered by him. The sparrow, though not remarkable for plumage or voice, cannot fall to the ground without the permission of our Heavenly Father, and then falls according to his laws. But we are of much more value than many sparrows. There is no place beyond the jurisdiction of our blessed Creator. There is no escaping, or being exiled out of his reach, nor beyond his eye. His laws are all around us. Nor is there in all the amplitude of the universe, a flower or a star, a spear of grass, an insect, an atom or a planet, that does not teach us the presence of God's laws, and illustrate the beauty of holiness, and the sublime lessons of the Cross. It is not then incredible that a beetle should have been commissioned to teach the way to a crown, and a little moss in an African desert should have preached the presence and goodness of God to a wearied and exhausted traveller when he lay down to die; but thus having his faith strengthened he put his trust in Him, who had made so tiny and beautiful a thing to grow in so vast and dreary a solitude, and revived and lived. It is an evidence of Divine goodness, that we may find "sermons in stones," theology in a crawling beetle, or in a desert moss, and "good in everything."

Eighth. As the success of faith rests upon the power of Him in whom it is exercised, *so it is instantaneous.* Christ is able and willing to save to the uttermost all that come to God through Him. And whosoever comes to Him, He will in no wise cast out. All our hope is in God. All our safety is in Him. The promise is, *if* we believe. The result of true faith is immutably certain. Christ is sufficient. So Jesus said unto the centurion, "Go thy way; and, as thou hast believed, so be it done unto thee." Our Lord condescended to comply with his terms. The centurion did not ask him to go to his house. He did not enter it. He asked Jesus simply to speak the word. Jesus did speak the word, and his servant was healed "in the selfsame hour." The recovery was immediate. So the poor leper was cured instantaneously, who had come saying, "Lord, if thou wilt, thou canst make me clean." "As thou hast believed, so be it done." Happily for us the simplicity of faith requires not the mastery of any system of doctrines nor the acquisition of any learned science. We are not to wait to know what faith is, but receive Christ as He is offered to us, and we have a Saviour. It is not by merely consenting to receive as true a system of doctrines, but by receiving the great

Redeemer himself that we are saved. The suddenness of the cure of the centurion's servant, the time when it happened, and the working of the miracle without any prescription or any kind of medical treatment had a convincing effect upon the people. And perhaps in no other case is the saving power, or the simplicity of faith, more happily illustrated than in this one. Faith is confidence, trust. It takes hold upon Him who is invisible and yet able to save to the uttermost all that come to Him. "If thou canst believe, all things are possible to him that believeth." "He that believeth shall be saved, and he that believeth not shall be damned." "He that believeth on the Son hath everlasting life, and he that believeth not shall not see life." "All things whatsoever ye ask in prayer, believing, ye shall receive." *Mark* xvi. 16; *John* iii. 36; *Matth.* xxi. 22; *Rom.* x.

But what are all these promises, if we no not feel our need of salvation? Is it true that you feel yourself to be a poor, miserable sinner? Then Jesus, in whom the centurion believed, has come to seek and save you. He offers himself to you as an Almighty Saviour. You are now called to repent and believe, and throw yourself into the outstretched arms of mercy. No matter how humble your employment may be—no matter how high and honorable it may be, you have only to accept of Jesus Christ as He is offered in the Gospel, and you will find peace and salvation. Have you received Him? Will you trust in Him?

V.

THE CENTURION COMMANDING AT THE CRUCIFIXION.

Now when the centurion, and they that were with him, watching Jesus, saw the earthquake, and those things that were done, they feared greatly, saying, Truly this was the Son of God.—*Matth.* xxvii. 54.

And when the centurion, which stood over against him, saw that he so cried out, and gave up the ghost, he said, Truly this man was the Son of God.—*Mark* xv. 39.

Now when the centurion saw what was done, he glorified God, saying, certainly this was a righteous man.—*Luke* xxiii. 47.

These verses manifestly describe the effect of the scenes of the crucifixion on the mind of Roman officer in command, and having charge of the execution of the sentence of death passed upon our Lord.

The centurion which stood over against him, in full sight of him, or standing in front of him. This was the natural and necessary position of the officer presiding at such an execution. And from it we see that the centurion had the circumstances of the crucifixion under his own personal observation. The whole scene was before him; and when he saw how Jesus expired after he had cried out, he exclaimed: "Truly this man was the Son of God." As if he had said, This is a most extraordinary case. This very man, against whom so much has been said, and who has been so cruelly treated, and so shamefully put to death as an impostor, must have been what he said he was—*the Son of God.*

This testimony, therefore, was the honest conviction of his own mind from what he himself had seen and heard. Nor was he alone. *Now when the centurion, and they that were with him, watching Jesus, saw the earthquake, and those things that were done, they feared greatly, saying, Truly this was the Son of God.*

Probably only four soldiers were employed in nailing Jesus to the cross; but a considerable number, perhaps his whole command, acted under the centurion as the guard, and watched him while he was hanging on the tree.

And thus it was that no part of the Gospel history is destitute of eye witnesses. The centurion is considered by some as having made his declaration *because* Christ spoke with a loud voice and expired, and that he simply expressed his astonishment that Christ should have had so much strength after such suffering and exhaustion. It was true that our Lord did not die of mere exhaustion, or from faintness and want of strength. For he gave up his life. He died voluntarily. Others, however, think the centurion meant to applaud our Lord for his constancy in calling upon the name of God to the last moment.

But it seems to us we are to take his confession as the utterance of a conviction produced in his mind by all that he saw and heard, by the miracles and the words of Christ applied to his conscience by the Spirit of God. More literally, *having thus cried out*, not having reference merely to the last expiring agony, but to the previous cry of "Eloi, Eloi, lama sabachthani." The sense seems to be this: when the centurion saw what was done, and heard what our Lord said, and felt the throes of the earthquake, and heard what had happened in the temple and among the dead in the neighboring tombs, and then turning to Jesus saw that he had given up the ghost, and while looking on his dead body as it hung there on the cross, where only the bodies of slaves and of the vilest wretches were wont to be found, he exclaimed: "Truly this man was the Son of God."

There is no contradiction between the statements of the three evangelists, neither as to what was said, nor what was omitted, nor as to whom what was said is attributed. *Matthew* says, "when the centurion and they that were with him, watching Jesus, saw the earthquake, and those things that were done, they feared greatly, saying," etc.; while *Mark* and *Luke* represent the centurion alone as speaking. They do not, however, say that the soldiers who were with the centurion did *not* speak. The probability is, they felt as their commanding officer did, and that they caught up his words and repeated them. Mere silence or omission in a contemporary writer is not a contradiction. And as to what was said, *Matthew* and *Mark* say: "Truly this man was the Son of God," while *Luke* says: "Certainly this was a righteous man." Now, on the supposition that the soldiers as well as the centurion united in the declaration, it is easy to see that it would be repeated many times, and sometimes might be slightly varied—that some would use one form of the phrase, and others another, expressive of the same idea. There is no intimation in the narratives that either of them exhausted all that was said, and that nothing else was said, or that the writers meant to do any such thing. The two forms of exclamation may have been used by different persons and at different times. There is, therefore, nothing strange in the fact that two evangelists should have recorded one, the third the other. In fact it is highly probable this would have been in conformity with custom; that when the centurion and a part of his command exclaimed, "Truly this man was the Son of God;" that the other part responded, saying: "Aye, certainly this was a righteous man." And besides, as we shall see, these exclamations mean substantially the same thing. For if he was a righteous man, he was the Son of God, for as a righteous man his professions must be honest and true, and we know that he claimed to be the Son of God; and if he was the Son of God, then he was righteous. The one expression explains the other. For as Jesus was crucified for claiming to be the Son of God, so if he was righteous, that is, innocent of any crime or wrong in what he said of himself, then he was unjustly condemned; and if so, then he was truly the Son of God. There is then no real discrepancy between the two expressions. What then is the meaning of the centurion's testimony concerning Jesus? Did he know the force of the terms he used? Some tell us that he knew no more what was meant by the appellation "Son of God," than the king of Babylon did when he said, "Lo! I see four men loose, walking in the midst of the fire; and the form of the fourth is like the Son of God." *Dan.* iii. 25. But however vague his idea may have been, he doubtless meant that the "Son of God" possessed superior excellence, supernatural goodness, and power divine. He knew that the controversy between our Lord and the Jews was about this very point. That his enemies denied that he was the Son of God, and charged him with blasphemy for saying that he was the Son of God. And he knew that Jesus still declared himself to be the Son of God. By his confession, therefore, he meant to say, whatever this man has said of himself is true. He is an innocent and righteous man, and whatever he meant by saying that he was the Son of God is true. The objection urged by some that the want of the article in the original makes the expression weak, only proves the correctness of our evangelist, and leaves the argument for our Lord's divinity quite as strong as it could have been with the article. It is true, the original text is literally without the article—*Son of God.* It is neither *the* Son of God, nor *a* Son of a God, nor of *the* God, but indefinitely, *Son of God;* and so doubtful is Dr. George Campbell as to the proper rendering of this text, that he professedly avoids any decision by translating it *God's Son*. But let us remember, on this point, that the evangelist is recording the language of a Roman officer, who has not been taught the Athanasian creed. How would a polytheist and a Roman express Son of God? *Filius Dei* is all he could say. As there is no definite article in the Latin language, he could not have used a more definite expression. The evangelist, therefore, was correct in giving his expression without the article. Nor does the omission of the article weaken the meaning of the centurion's testimony. In the passage where the disciples came to Jesus after he had quelled the storm, and worshipped him, saying, Truly thou art the Son of God, the article is wanting, just as in the passage before us.

Indeed, some of the ablest *Socinian* critics have admitted that the use or omission of the article in the original here proves nothing, for that the expression means exactly the same thing with or without the article. It is true that *Son of God*, as the Polytheistic Romans understood theology, would have signified no more than a *hero, an eminent or divine person,* but in this case the centurion is not speaking of the opinion of heathen Polytheists, but in reference to a specific case and a specific charge. His phraseology was certainly suggested to him by, and adopted from, what he had heard of the charge alleged against the extraordinary person that was then hanging dead before him upon the cross. The whole connection requires such an application of this testimony. The meaning is definite. This is frequently the case where the article is omitted, but in this case it could not have been used. The centurion being a heathen and using the Latin language, meant to say, as nearly as he could, that Jesus was just what he claimed to be. His testimony cannot, therefore, with any fairness, be interpreted in a mere polytheistic sense, but according to the issue then pending between our Lord and his adversaries. It is impossible to conclude that such a man as this centurion was ignorant of the main points of the dispute. As a Roman officer on duty in the ecclesiastical capital of Judea, and near the proconsular judgment seat, he must have been a man of some considerable education and intelligence, and must have known that the Jews worshipped Jehovah as the one living and true God, and he must also have known that the ecclesiastical charge on which Jesus was crucified was blasphemy, and that this charge was made against him by implication from his claiming to be the Son of God, or a partaker of the nature of the supreme divinity; and he must also have felt satisfied in his own mind that the Supreme God, who was the author of these prodigies by which they were then so deeply impressed, intended them to attest the truth of the claim set up by the sufferer, and thus to vindicate his innocence. And it was in view of all these facts—under all these circumstances—that the Roman officer in command on the day of the crucifixion meant to declare that it was his conviction, without knowing or caring or troubling himself about the ceremonies and creed of the Jews, that Jesus, in whatever sense he claimed to be divine, or to be the Son of God, was to be believed. He meant to take part with Jesus as against his accusers. He meant to affirm most emphatically what the Jews denied, and to confirm what Jesus had professed concerning himself. It was not, therefore, a mere random heathen expression of admiration, but an earnest, full-hearted confession, as far as he understood the subject, that he believed Jesus was the Son of God. The adverb *truly* is not without its force in this passage. In the original it is emphatic. Certainly, without doubt. It is no longer to be disputed. *This was the Son of God*—in antithesis to the assertions made by our Lord himself, when he said, He was the Son of God. And let us remember that the whole object of the Gospel is to bring us to make this same confession—to believe in our heart that Jesus Christ is the Son of God, and when truly made, this confession is salvation. Let us now attend to *the circumstances under which this testimony was given.* Matthew says: "When the centurion, and they that were with him, watching Jesus, saw the earthquake, and those things that were done, they feared greatly, saying, Truly this was the

Son of God." This language plainly implies that there were other supernatural occurrences —other things besides the earthquake that made a deep impression on the centurion's mind. As the testimony of a layman on religious matters about which he is sufficiently conversant to give an opinion, may be more impartial than that of a priest or minister, so the centurion's testimony is valuable, because of its manifest impartiality. He was not a member of the Sanhedrim. He was no ecclesiastic. Whatever prejudices he may have had on the subject of religion were doubtless diverse to the claims of Jesus, and he was without any private or personal spite. He was in every respect capable of judging calmly and impartially of the evidence before him. And he was a soldier, which, however, does not disqualify him from giving testimony, nor from being pious. Soldiers and sailors are proverbially honest, open and candid, quick to apprehend what they see and hear, and ready to express their convictions. Their lives often depend upon their quickness of apprehension and upon the accuracy with which they can see and hear, and the courage and promptitude with which they can act. Necessity and habit develop these faculties. And we see how they were employed in the case before us. While the priests, ecclesiastics and members of the Sanhedrim were so blinded by prejudice and enraged by passion that they could neither see nor hear the proofs of Jesus' messiahship, the centurion perceived them, and was bold enough to say, "Truly this was the Son of God." He did not ask whether it was safe or expedient to do so or not, but, soldierlike, speaks out the sentiment of his heart. The persons then making this confession were the Roman officer in command and the guard of soldiers under him who executed the sentence of execution. As Gentiles, they knew not the Scriptures, and their testimony is an undesigned admission of their truth.

The direct or apparent means of their conviction were the earthquake and the wonderful things that accompanied the crucifixion. Nature expressed her abhorrence of the guilt of man, and her sympathy with the illustrious sufferer This was admitted even by heathens. And even now God makes both his judgments and his mercies ministers for working conviction of sin. The manifestations of their conviction were twofold, namely: *their alarm* and *their confession*. Guilt makes men cowards. They were terrified lest the earth in its heavings should open her jaws and swallow them up. Their noble confession was a testimony extorted from enemies on the very point then in dispute. The issue plainly made was: Is Christ the Son of God or not? *Calvin* does not think the centurion was converted to God, but was only for a moment made the herald of Christ's divinity; just as men, under some sudden and transitory impulse, are struck with the fear of God as they see some alarming display of his power; but not having the root of the matter in them, they soon cease to have any feeling on the subject. In this instance, however, this great theologian and commentator does not seem to have considered the text and its parallels in the original. For *Matthew* says the centurion and those that were with him *were greatly terrified—ephobethesan sphrodra;* and *Luke* says the centurion glorified God—*edoxase ton Theon.* But it has, indeed, sometimes happened that persons have been led to utter words that contained more meaning than they knew or intended. Indeed, it is an open question whether or not men under the prophetic ecstasy understood what they were saying at all. Balaam's prophecy is a case in point. What he said was true, but it is not clear that he was the willing agent of its utterance, or that he fully comprehended what he said. And so Caiaphas declared that it was "expedient for us that one man should die for the people, and that the whole nation perish not." *John* xviii. 14. In this remarkable declaration there is a great and precious truth which Caiaphas did not mean to express, for of it there is no reason to suppose he had any conception. What he did mean to say is the dangerous doctrine that the end justifies the means—the unprincipled assertion that expediency is more than right or justice. And so also when Pilate caused the trilingual inscription to be put over our Lord's head, "Jesus of Nazareth, the King of the Jews," he had but an imperfect idea of his regal character—in fact, did not see his true glory at all; yet his inscription was a most important declaration of our Lord's true character. And so, when the infuriated Jews cried out, his blood be upon us and upon our children, they did not comprehend the terrible meaning of the vengeance they invoked upon themselves. And thus it may be, the centurion did not comprehend the meaning of his own confession. His words may mean more than he knew or intended.

Nothing is known with any certainty about this centurion beyond what is contained in the text. The exclamation may have been the expression of a momentary feeling, and may have been forgotten, though we trust the traditions of the ancient church are correct, and that he became a Christian and a saint. We understand *Luke's* expression, *glorified God*, to mean, that they gave God praise by their confession that Jesus was his Son, and so manifested forth his glory. They *feared greatly*—were intensely excited by the scenes transpiring. And may we not suppose the spirit of God opened their hearts and that they made confession of their sins to God, and deprecated his wrath when they declared that Jesus was most certainly his Son? From such a view of their case, as well as from the fact that they must have been included in the Saviour's intercessory prayer—and "Him the Father always heareth"—"Father forgive them;" it seems to us we are authorized to conclude that their convictions at the crucifixion resulted in their conversion, and that they became followers of him whom they had nailed to the cross or seen crucified as a malefactor.

Previous to this moment, however, there is no reason to suppose that this centurion had expressed any faith in or friendship for Christ. The general impression in regard to him is, that he was the Roman officer in command, under whose orders the crown of thorns, and the arraying in the purple robe and the smiting and the spitting on our Lord's face had been permitted. It is not probable that he commanded such deeds of cruelty and outrage to be done; but he did not prevent them. As the officer appointed by Pilate to execute his sentence, it was by him the cross was prepared, by his order the nails were driven through the hands and the feet of Jesus. He was the officer presiding at the execution. His confession, therefore, when the bloody deed was done, and he looked upon the dead body and said, "Certainly this was a righteous man"—"Truly this was the Son of God," is the more remarkable. We find Matthew's account more full than Mark's. He says: "Now, when the centurion and they that were with him, watching Jesus, saw the earthquake and those things that were done, they feared greatly, saying, Truly this was the Son of God." It seems to be implied here that many wonderful things were done in that solemn hour; many of which are not named or described. Among these things we know were the rending of the veil of the temple from top to bottom; the rending of the rocks; the opening of the graves and the coming forth of many of the saints; the supernatural darkness; and a great earthquake. Nature seemed in convulsive throes, and the last judgment at hand. It is also clear from the evangelist's record, that the soldiers shared the centurion's profound emotions. They felt as he did; yes, the very men who had spit upon his face and smote him on the cheek, and had mocked and derided him for the purpose of pleasing the Jewish populace—the very men by whose hands he had been crucified, felt as their commanding officer did, when he said, *Truly this man was the Son of God. Certainly this was a righteous man.* It is true, that the centurion and the soldiers with him could not have witnessed all these wonderful things themselves. They were either wholly ignorant of some of them, or knew only of them by report; but they heard the crashing of the rocks and timbers, and were sensible of the supernatural darkness and of the earthquake's throes. Then we must also take into the account just here what the centurion had seen and heard that day. He was accustomed to the shock of battle and the crash of arms, to scenes of blood. He had doubtless witnessed many an execution before, but never one like this. He had some knowledge of the alleged crimes of the sufferer. The presumption in his mind no doubt at first was that he was guilty, and deserved all he had to endure. But through the day he must have been impressed with something supernatural in the bearing of the victim. He saw him arraigned, he heard his defence; saw him insulted and tortured, and nailed to the cross, and that still he opened not his mouth, that He bore all without a murmur. He was surprised that the storm of abuse and blasphemy hurled at him was not resented. Nor could he have failed to know something of the admonition: "Daughters of Jerusalem, weep not for me, but for yourselves, and for your children."

And he must have known that Jesus had said to the penitent thief with whom he was crucified, "Verily I say unto thee, to-day thou shalt be with me in paradise." And he must have heard the prayer, "Father, forgive them, for they know not what they do." A prayer that embraced himself and his soldier band. Nor did the words: " Eloi, Eloi, lama sabachthani; My God, my God, why hast thou forsaken me?" and "It is finished," escape his ears, nor the expiring words: "Father, into thy hands I commend my spirit." These particulars were unusual. They were fresh. They could not have been unnoticed by a Roman centurion on duty. No other crucified man, Hebrew or Gentile, innocent or guilty, had ever displayed such a spirit, or exhibited so sublime a picture of magnanimity and benevolence. The centurion's confession was, therefore, produced by the pressure of external occurrences, and by the conviction forced upon his mind by reflecting on what he had learned—what he had heard and seen. But what is the meaning of the exclamation, "Certainly this was a righteous man?" What did he mean by *righteous?* He was not a Jew. There is no evidence that he was even a Jewish proselyte. Nor could he have known much, if anything, concerning the expected Jewish Messiah. The sources of his knowledge as to what constituted a righteous man must have been, not Revelation—not the laws of Moses; but common sense, the light of natural conscience, and the force of his military education as a Roman soldier and officer, aided by the glimmering light of tradition. He must have had some distinct conviction that there was a difference between right and wrong. And he must have felt that there was a difference between Jesus and the other two malefactors crucified with him. The two thieves made no impression on his mind. He saw nothing in them that was remarkable. One of them, indeed, professed penitence, but that was not unusual. Nor is it probable that they died without many outcries; one of them at least uttered bitter blasphemies to the very last. But Jesus, on the other hand, as a sheep before her shearers is dumb, so he opened not his mouth against those that crucified him. From the whole, then, we conclude the centurion meant to say: this man is certainly innocent of the crimes alleged against him. He is certainly the Son of God. The conviction on his mind was very strong that superhuman excellence and power were concentrated in this man. Nor is this view unnatural to a heathen. For they were familiar with making gods of heroes, and with the descent of the deities to earth, and with their assuming or dwelling in human forms. And nature had spoken here in such a manner as to show that the event was an extraordinary one.

Nor is the fact that Jesus was executed under a judicial sentence any conclusive evidence against the correctness of the centurion's declaration, that he certainly was a righteous man. For many a judicial murder has been committed. Many an innocent man has been put to death by violence and even with the authority of the laws. The earth has drunken the blood of many martyrs, and yet the heavens gave no signs at the time that a righteous God would avenge their blood. It was a proper, a very natural inference, therefore, of the centurion, that the supernatural phenomena that he witnessed were to be understood as the testimony of Nature in behalf of the innocence and divinity of Jesus. The expression in *Luke* seems to be a reference to the message of Pilate's wife, who, when Jesus was before her husband, sent to him on the judgment seat, saying: "Have thou nothing to do with that just man." This the centurion, from his position, was very likely to have heard, and coming to the conclusion that she was right, he cries out as Pilate's wife has said: "Truly, this man was a righteous man." Jesus was righteous both as to the precepts and the penalty of the Divine law. He perfectly obeyed it. He was without sin. And he endured its penalty for his people. The law of God was in his heart. It was his delight to do it. He fulfilled all righteousness. None of his adversaries could convict him of sin. In regard to the whole law of God he was faultless. He knew no sin, and yet he was a sin offering for us. As a righteous man he deserved no suffering, but the "Lord laid on him the iniquities of us all. He was wounded for our transgressions, he was bruised for our iniquities; the chastisements of our peace was upon him; and with his stripes we are healed." "He gave himself for us an offering and a sacrifice to God of a sweet-smelling savor." "He bare our sins in his own body on the tree." "He suffered the just for the unjust, that he might bring us to God." Little, then, did this Roman officer know when he declared that Jesus was a righteous man, that he was declaring the fulfilment of inspired prophecies, and pointing him out to us as the RIGHTEOUS ONE, the JUST ONE, and THE HOLY, in whom we have righteousness and salvation. But what is the meaning of his declaration—"Truly this was the Son of God?" This is not the first time that we meet with this appellation as applied to Christ. A voice from heaven proclaimed at his baptism—"This is my beloved Son." Devils have also said, "We know thee who thou art: Thou art the Son of God;" and we have heard his disciples confessing amid the tempest on the sea, "of a truth thou art the Son of God." And in John we find the Jews charging it upon him as blasphemy—that calling himself the Son of God, he had made himself God. The Jews said: "He made himself equal with God because he made himself the Son of God." *John* xix. 7. And in *Luke*, we read: "Then said they all, Art thou then the Son of God? And he said unto them, ye say that I am." That is, what you say is true. I am what you call me. And then the Jews, said, "What need we any further witness? for we ourselves have heard of his own mouth." Now, it must have been in reference to this accusation that the centurion made his declaration. It is as if he had said, You call it blasphemy for this man to assume to be the Son of God, and you may prefer a murderer, but in spite of the verdict of your Sanhedrim and of the decrees of your synagogues, I tell you, He is the Son of God. Let us see, then, if this declaration of the centurion is true. Was he justified in saying that Jesus was truly the Son of God? We think he was, *first*, because Jesus meets the prophetic requirements of the promised Messiah. According to the Scriptures, the Messiah was to come of the seed of the woman, and of Abraham's seed through the tribe of Judah and of the family of David. And he was to come while the second temple was standing, and while the sceptre was still in Judah, and a lawgiver and a king was yet among them, and he was to be born in Bethlehem, and he was to work such miracles and preach such doctrines and suffer such things, and was to die with malefactors and make his grave with the rich, and to rise again from the dead, and to live and reign forever as Head over all things. In short, every promise, every prophecy, everything required according to the Scriptures to constitute the proofs that he was the Messiah is found in the coming, life, words and works of Jesus Christ. The promises and prophecies are all fulfilled in him. *Second*, the perfection of his character is such as none but the Son of God could exhibit, and its description such as none but inspired men could write. There was no such character for them to copy from. There was none before; there has been none since like it. The character which the Evangelists have given to Christ proves, therefore, both the divine inspiration of their narratives, and that one so holy, so perfect, was truly *the Son of God*.

It can hardly be necessary to dwell at length upon the attributes displayed in his life that prove his portrait to be divine. His meekness was united with ineffable majesty. He made others rich, but remained himself so poor that he had to work a miracle to pay his taxes. The Lord of angels and of all worlds, he could yet say: "The foxes have holes and the birds of the air have nests; but the Son of Man hath not where to lay his head," nor was his humility any less conspicuous than his majesty. Witness his example when he would teach his followers to be humble and self-denying. At the last supper, he took a towel and girded himself and washed the feet of his disciples. Observe, also, not only the perfection of his character, but the extraordinary wisdom that is seen in all his actions throughout his whole life. Begin with the record of his conference with the doctors in the temple, and study his words till he said, "It is finished," and you will find that "never man spake like this man."

And his piety was as remarkable as his wisdom. Being truly man as well as God, it cannot be improper to speak of the piety of Jesus. He had a creed, an experience, and a practice in his religion. And in all these things he was an example. We should believe what he believed and follow his example in our conduct. He was truly a man in everything except sin. And in trying to get a full face view of Him, we must never lose sight of his humanity. We must keep in mind his estate of humiliation as well as his estate of exaltation. How he suffered and died, and how he arose from the dead, and now lives and reigns in glory. And *his beneficence* was unceasing. His miracles were never for himself merely. They were not wrought merely to display his power, nor to confound his enemies. They were as full of grace as of omnipotence. He healed the sick, the lame, the blind and the deaf. He raised the dead. He preached glad tidings to the poor. Nor was his sympathy less remarkable than his beneficence. When the disciples rebuked those mothers who brought their ragged and almost naked children to him, supposing it an insult, or that he ought not to be troubled with them, mark his conduct. He said, suffer little children to come unto me, and forbid them not; for of such is the kingdom of heaven. And he took them into his arms, and put his hands upon them, and blessed them, saying, of such is the kingdom of heaven.

The history of our Lord's last moments and of the centurion's confession, may be collected and condensed from a harmony of all the evangelists into the following narrative: As he breathed his last the veil of the temple in the presence of the officiating high-priest, who was engaged at the evening sacrifice, was miraculously rent from top to bottom; and the earth did quake and the rocks rent; and the graves in the rocks were opened, and many bodies of the saints which slept arose, and came out of the graves after his resurrection. That is, the graves were opened by the earthquake at our Lord's death, but the dead did not arise and come into the city till his resurrection. As the rending of the veil of the temple was typical of the opening of the gospel kingdom to all nations, so the resurrection at this time of a number of saints from the dead, was a demonstration that the power of death and of the grave was broken. Our Lord's victory, therefore, over death and the grave was complete. "*And when the centurion and they that were with him, watching Jesus, which stood over against him, saw that he so cried out, and gave up the ghost—saw the earthquake, and those things that were done, he glorified God, saying, Certainly this was a righteous man—Truly this man was the Son of God.*" Bengel well says in this place: "Great commotions in created things went on, in continuous succession, from the moment of Christ's death to his resurrection, exerting their influence especially in the kingdom of things invisible."

It is well here to observe the difference of the effect produced on different persons by the same things. The prodigies accompanying our Lord's death convinced the heathen officer and his guard of soldiers that Christ was the Son of God, but left the Jewish doctors and rulers more confirmed in their obstinacy and unbelief. Their prejudices against Jesus were so invincible, that they could be convinced neither by the miracles nor doctrines, nor by the manner of his life, nor by his demeanor in death, nor by the utterance of nature in attestation of his innocence. Truly none are so blind as they that are so filled with prejudice that they will not see. But nevertheless, wisdom is justified in all her children and in all her ways. For all God's administrations to us have an effect. They either soften or harden; save or destroy. Every mercy and every judgment is a saviour of life unto life, or of death unto death. It is astonishing how great an amount of incidental or undesigned evidence might be gathered up for the truth of Christianity. The undesigned coincidences of the sacred writers themselves would form quite an overwhelming mass of evidence to prove that they were capable, honest, truth-telling eye-witnesses. The testimony corroborative also from enemies is exceedingly strong. We have before us the testimony of a Roman officer and of his command of the time and the place of our Lord's crucifixion, that he was a righteous man and the Son of God. Even devils on several different occasions during his lifetime made the same confession. Peter and the other disciples had also made the same declaration. Pilate and Herod said there was no fault in him. He had done nothing worthy of death. Pilate's wife declared him to be an innocent and just person. And so Judas himself testified that he had betrayed innocent blood. All sorts of people in many lands, and through all past ages, have borne testimony to Jesus Christ, that he is the Son of God, and the Saviour of the world. How then can we escape if we believe not in him? It is remarkable how often in the Scriptures we find the material universe, by means of physical occurrences, giving witness of the events which accompanied the utterance of great moral or spiritual truth. This was the case at the giving of the Law at Mount Sinai; and the vision of angels at the birth of Jesus is a similar instance of the sympathy of the spiritual world with man's history. In the great turning points of man's moral history, the material universe appears in peculiar connection with him. As at the birth, so at the death of Jesus, physical phenomena attest the sympathy of material things with human redemption. The supernatural darkness, the rent veil, the torn rocks, and the earthquake, are but expressions by which the God of Nature through physical prodigies made known his abhorrence of sin and the greatness of the salvation that is offered to us, through our Lord Jesus Christ, to whom be glory for ever, AMEN.

VI.

THE CENTURION OF CESAREA.

There was a certain man in Cesarea called Cornelius, a centurion of the band called the Italian band, a devout man, and one that feared God with all his house, which gave much alms to the people, and prayed to God always.—Acts x. 1–2.

Having read the whole of the interesting chapter from which the above text is taken, we invite you to consider:

1.—*The subject of Divine Grace here introduced—His Antecedents and Circumstances.*

His name was Cornelius; a name distinguished among the Romans, especially as connected with the Scipios and Scyllas; by birth a Gentile and most probably a Roman, and by profession a soldier, and by position an officer stationed at this time with his company at Cesarea, in command of a part of the Roman forces, then holding Palestine in subjection.

This Cesarea was called *Cesarea Palestina*, to distinguish it from *Cesarea Philippi*, which was a city about one hundred and twenty miles north of Jerusalem and near the sources of the Jordan in the mountains of Lebanon. *Cesarea Palestina* was formerly called Strato's tower. It was on the sea shore about sixty miles from Jerusalem; built by Herod the Great in honor of Augustus Cæsar, twenty-two years before the birth of Christ. It was a city of great beauty and wealth, and at this time the seat of the civil government of Judea, as Jerusalem was of the ecclesiastical. It was distinguished for its semi-circular mole, which was one of the most stupendous works of antiquity. Within its inclosure a large fleet could ride in perfect security in all weathers. The stones of this mole were immense blocks and brought from a great distance, and sunk twenty fathoms in the sea. It was chiefly inhabited by Gentiles, though some thousands of Jews lived there. Vespasian made it a Roman colony, exempting it from capitation and ground taxes. In the New Testament it is several times referred to besides in the case before us. Here Philip the evangelist resided for some time, and Paul spent the space of perhaps two years here, on his way to Rome, and from this city he sailed when he commenced his voyage to Italy, during which he was wrecked at Malta. Here he made his speech before Festus and Agrippa, and here, in the amphitheatre, Herod Agrippa was smitten to death for not giving God the glory. It was a renowned city, and the seat of the Roman Court until Judea ceased to be a Roman province. In the commencement of the wars with the Jews, twenty thousand Jews of Cesarea were massacred by the Gentiles. A most graphic and thrilling account of this massacre is given in one of the works of the late Dr. Ware, of Boston. This city is noted in later times as the birth-place and episcopate of the great Church historian of the fourth century, Eusebius. A pile of ruin, now called Kaiserah, marks the site of this once courtly city. It is seldom visited. The present inhabitants of the old castle and surrounding ruins, which cover a great space, are jackals, wild boars, snakes, lizards and scorpions.

A centurion of the band called the Italian band. *Band* means cohort or division of the Roman army, consisting sometimes of four or six hundred, or of a thousand footmen, of whom the chief was called a tribune or marshal, corresponding to our colonel of a regiment. These cohorts were subdivided into companies of a hundred each, the captain of which was called the centurion. Usually a legion was composed of five bands, that is, of about five thousand infantry. *Italian band* means that they were soldiers from Italy, as we say, " the New York regiment," or " the Louisiana legion," or as English officers in India are distinguished from the Sepoys. An old inscription mentions " the cohort of Italian volunteers which is in Syria." Arrian also speaks of the foot soldiers of the Italian band. Though the Roman armies were increased by levies from the conquered provinces, their chief strength was drawn from the mother country. Soldiers from Italy no doubt claimed a preëminence over those enlisted from other places. Josephus speaks of Cesarian cohorts as distinguished from the *Italian legion*. And even if, as some think, the Italian legion of Tacitus and Josephus was not formed at this time, all admit that there was an *Italian cohort*, which answers quite as well as the original. It was probably the life-guard of the Roman governor or proconsul who resided there, and called the *Italian cohort* by way of distinction from the others, who were raised from the provinces. For it was the custom of the emperors to distribute their forces so as to occupy the chief cities of the empire by garrisons, in order that sudden uproars, insurrections or invasions might be met and at once put down.

The *second* verse is an amplification of the completeness of the centurion's character. He was a perfect gentleman. He feared God, regarded man, and took the proper care of his household. He kept both tables of the divine law. His faith was orthodox, and his life proved it to be fruitful. He had a church in his house. Its members were obedient unto him in godliness.

A devout man—according to some, means that he was a religious heathen. Others, and this is perhaps the general opinion, say that he was a "proselyte of the gate," that is, had renounced idolatry, and had so far embraced the Jewish religion, that he kept the seven precepts of Noah, and was kindly disposed to the Jews, but had not yet been circumcised. The arguments in favor of this last opinion are:

First. It is said he *feared God*, whereas if he had become a full proselyte, he would have been numbered with the Hebrews and have been spoken of as a Jew. *Second.* His hours of prayer were according to Hebrew custom. And it is clear also that he was acquainted with the Old Testament, for when Peter preaches to him, we find him appealing to Hebrew Scriptures for proofs that Jesus is the Messiah. This implies his acquaintance with them and belief in them, at least so far as to receive them as true historical records. And then, *third*, he was kindly disposed to the Jews. It is not absolutely certain, however, that he was "a proselyte of the gate." Wetstein says he *feared* God and *worshipped* Him as the true God, distinguishing correctly between the original terms for *fear* and *worship*, which are not the same, and concludes that the meaning is, he feared and acknowledged God as the one only living and true God, and that he regulated his life by the rule of nature, and not by Mosaic precepts, and that, consequently, we are not to look upon him as a Jewish proselyte, but as a pious Gentile. This seems to us the correct opinion. He was at least a Gentile by birth, name and profession, and he was a *devout man*, whether he had ever been recognized as a convert to the Hebrew religion or not. Another (*fourth*) reason, however, which we think conclusive that he had not professed himself a convert to Judaism, is, that as a Roman the laws prohibited him from receiving any new or strange religion; and certainly he was as yet a Roman officer, and holding an honored position in the government. The whole force of the narrative seems to us lost, if he were a Jewish convert.

The intent of the history is to show how the Gospel Church was opened to Gentiles without the intervention of Judaism.

The character of this man is more exalted, if, as we look at his uprightness, courtesy toward men and devotion to God, we remember who he was, whence he was, and his peculiar temptations. Brought up in heathen superstition, he has already been converted to the worship of the true God; to the worship of Jehovah, the God of the Jews, who were a despised and conquered people. The Hebrews were at this time held in peculiar contempt, and it shows the strength of this man's character, that he could rise superior to prejudice, and appreciate the excellence of a religion that was held by a people that his country esteemed so execrable. And then again, he was not only a soldier, but an Italian officer in a conquered country, and under such circumstances, the Roman cohorts often ran over the provinces like hungry wolves, making a prey of all they could get. "They had," says Calvin, "for the most part no more religion than beasts; they had as great care of innocency as cut-throats, for which cause the virtues of Cornelius deserve the greater commendation, in that leading a soldier's life, which was at that time most corrupt, he served God holily, and lived amongst men without doing any hurt or injury." His piety is, moreover, the more remarkable because the lives of the leading professors of the Hebrew religion at that time were anything else than commendable. Instead of alluring the heathen among them to the worship of the true God by their sincerity, humility and charity, the Scribes and Pharisees were censorious, proud, cold, formal and hypocritical. But he *feared God with all his house*, that is, family. This means that he governed and instructed them. True piety is always accompanied by a sincere desire for the salvation of others, especially of those with whom we are closely connected, or for whose welfare we feel especially responsible. However it may have been with other Roman officers, this one, in fearing God himself, was successful in making his sentiments and conduct prevail over his household. Nor was his influence confined to his own house—for he *gave much alms to the people*. Alms here are used by a figure of speech for all that a charitable and bountiful man, with the love of God in his heart, would do for his fellow-men. "Blessed is he that considereth the poor: the Lord will deliver him in the time of trouble."—*Psalm* xli. 1.

And prayed to God always—that is, continually. He observed the regular seasons of prayer—did not neglect the morning and evening sacrifices. "Rejoice," says Paul, "in hope; patient in tribulation; continuing instant in prayer." And our Lord has taught us that men ought always to pray and not to faint. *Luke* xviii., and also 1 *Thess.* vi. Daniel prayed three times every day. The early Christians were careful to pray at the third, sixth and ninth hours; that is, at nine, twelve and three. It is also to be remembered that Cornelius, as a soldier and an officer on duty, had much to do, and many hindrances to overcome; but while he was faithful, punctual and prompt in the duties of his office, he could also find time for prayer. His heart was always in a praying mood. If we incline our ear unto wisdom, and apply our heart to understanding; if we cry after knowledge, and lift up our voice for understanding; if we seek it as silver and search for wisdom as for hidden treasures; then we shall know the peace of the Lord, and find the knowledge of God. *Prov.* ii. 2–5. Blessed are they that keep his testimonies, and that seek him with the whole heart. *Ps.* cxix. 2.

It is a happy remark of *Chrysostom, the golden mouth,* that the Ethiopian eunuch, treasurer of Queen Candace, and the Centurion Cornelius, are not mentioned because of their official rank and station, but because their official duties and rank did not hinder them from serving God. If there is not as much piety, therefore, in the army and navy as we should expect from the education, profession and position of the officers and men, it is not for the want of examples in both ancient and modern times. It may indeed be true, that the precariousness of life amid the dangers of war, instead of awakening the mind to a proper preparation for eternity, is turned into an argument for neglecting religion, if not made a plea for dissipation. It is a well known fact that in some of our cities nearness of the graveyard raises a suspicion of low morals—that plagues and epidemics, instead of reforming a city, have been noted for prevailing violence and licentiousness. We know historically that this has been true of Jerusalem, Bagdad, Cairo, London, and of some cities on our own continent. A most remarkable instance of this is seen in the history of Florence in the fourteenth century, when the plague almost depopulated the city and surrounding country; and yet the morals of the survivors grew worse and worse as the plague raged the more and more deadly. The tales of Boccaccio illustrate that familiarity with sickness and death, exposure to shame and peril, does not convert men. Nor are the judgments of God miracles of themselves sufficient to bring men to salvation. They always harden rather than soften, unless accompanied by the grace of God. It is at least painfully true that the hazards of military life do not always make men mindful of their duty to God. Still, as a class, they are not excluded from the offer of the Gospel. Nor is it right that prejudices against any class of men or profession should be a hindrance in their way to salvation. It is certainly not an impossibility to belong to the military profession and at the same time be truly pious. It may require much courage to dwell in camps and resist temptations to evil doing; yet it is hardly worse than to be a lawyer or a merchant. Opportunities for sinning and temptations to wrong-doing are in all occupations and in every one's path. But a long list of military and naval heroes could be given who were as remarkable for their piety as for their success in war. It is never proper to allow our prejudices to be excited against men *as classes* or professions that are not in themselves sinful.

VII.

THE CENTURION OF CESAREA CONTINUED.

HAVING considered this Roman officer as a subject of divine grace—his antecedents and circumstances, we proceed:

2.—*The Means or Agents employed to bring about and develop his Conversion to Christianity.*

In his case we are not told when he was "effectually called," or regenerated; but we may see clearly that his regeneration was before his conversion. In fact, he was pious before he knew what conversion meant. He was devout and feared God, and gave alms and prayed always and constrained his household to do likewise, before he knew anything of the Gospel as a system of divine grace. Not, indeed, before his heart was under divine influence, but before he knew anything of the proofs that Jesus was the Messiah, and that salvation was only through him. A child eats bread and is nourished by it long before he knows how to analyze the bread and call it by its chemical names. And we breathe the air, and live upon it, and may never be able to describe it philosophically. So in Cornelius we find the evidences of divine grace before he has learned how or whence he received it. How far God sends his Holy Spirit to open the hearts of the heathen, who are without the Gospel or his written Word, we cannot say. It is not for us, however, to limit the Holy One. And though divine influence is to be expected chiefly in connection with the Word read and preached, yet the Holy Ghost is not dependent on the Scriptures. The holy Scriptures have not created the Holy Spirit. On the contrary, the Scriptures were written by men moved thereto by the Holy Spirit. We dare not affirm—we do not believe that God cannot convert and save men without his written Word. Still, it is true that it is chiefly by his Word read and preached that men are converted and saved.

In Cornelius, we can see how his mind might be led through the whole process of conviction for sin, and to faith and repentance without his ever having learned to distinguish theologically between regeneration and conversion—conviction natural and saving, repentance legal and repentance evangelical. A man may plough and plant and reap, who knows nothing of the scientific nomenclature of agricultural chemistry. We must not suppose, however, that Cornelius was a pious man at or from his natural birth; nor that he was made pious by the mere culture of military discipline. However much his education may have done for him—still his military code did not produce his piety. The efficient cause of his piety was supernatural before he ever heard of Peter or the Holy Ghost, and it was produced by means. And in his case, THE MEANS were the light of Nature, the teachings of conscience and of tradition, and the direct influence of the spirit of God by and with and through these instruments upon his heart. We do not, therefore, look for, nor do we find in the wonderful narrative before us any metaphysical or formal account of this man's regeneration. All we have is a very brief statement of the effects of his regeneration, namely, his conversion to Christ. That is, of his embracing Christianity as preached by the Apostle. Now, as the power of magnetism is one thing, and the *actual turning* of the needle to the pole is another; and as the law, power, nature, or whatever it is that is in the sunflower that causes its attraction toward the sun, is quite a different thing from, but essential to the flower's turning its face toward and following the sun: so regeneration and conversion are inseparable, but distinct. Cornelius was a pious man, but not converted to Christianity before he heard Peter preach. God had touched his heart, and now the effect is seen.

THE MEANS OF HIS CONVERSION, then, were extraordinary and ordinary—supernatural and common. Human and divine agency wrought effectually and in perfect harmony, and without any violence to the freedom of the human will. And the agencies employed in this case were precisely the same that are employed now in every essential, though the details and minor agents are different.

He saw in a vision. Verse 3. Eichhorn, Rosenmuller and others say in a *dream.* And Heinrich will have it nothing but a common dream, which, however, Storr has ably refuted. The language does not suggest a dream. It was not the time for sleep or dreams. It was at the hour of prayer, the ninth hour, when it was full daylight, that the angelic vision appeared. Cornelius was not only awake, but engaged in the most solemn prayer of the day.

Commentators have enumerated seven ways in which God formerly revealed himself to men, namely: by dreams; by apparitions while they were awake; by visions while they slept; by a voice from heaven; by the Urim; by inspiration or auricular revelation, and by ecstasy or rapture, by which a man was snatched up into heaven, which Lightfoot says was "of all other modes the most excellent." See *Rev.* i. 10; 2 *Cor.* xii. 2.

Evidently—manifestly, not dimly or doubtfully—he was conscious of everything and perfectly sure of what he saw. It was not likely that a Roman officer, at such an hour, or under such circumstances, could have been deceived or imposed upon.

An angel of God from heaven—one of those that attend around his throne as his ministers, waiting to do his will. The same angel, probably, who appeared to Manoah, Moses, Daniel, and Zachariah. This messenger from the world of superhuman spirits appeared clothed as a man; generally at first mistaken for a man of God, that is, one of the prophets. So Manoah thought at first the angel that appeared to him was a man of God. The popular idea that angels always appeared with wings is erroneous. The cherubim and seraphim had wings, and probably it is from them this idea that angelic visitors to earth are always represented as having wings has obtained. But the angels that appeared to Abraham to tell him about Sodom and Gomorrah had no wings. There is something unartistic and absurd in the pictures of Old Testament angels that we sometimes see—walking on the earth and with men and like men, except that their wings are somehow folded up on their backs or over their shoulders. The true representation of angelic visitors to man is to clothe them in the ordinary dress of the religious teachers of the people to whom they were sent.

The vision was to him as an oracle from God—not in the night season, but in open daylight—and accompanied with such seals or assurances, or marks of certainty imprinted upon his mind, as left him in no doubt of its truthfulness. It was not an illusion, but a reality. It was a vision from God. The fear that seized him when the vision appeared, was that of a brave and sensible man. Perceiving that it was God that had sent the vision, and that he had now to deal with Him, he very properly asked: *What is it, Lord?* *Lord* here is no more than our *Sir*. And the angel answered: "Thy prayers and thine alms have come up for a memorial before God." *Verse* 4.

Come up is an allusion to the offering up of incense, whose fragrance and smoke ascended toward heaven, and were then considered as acceptable to God.

For a memorial—that is, are remembered before God. The force of this assurance lies in the fact, that as he was a Gentile, had not been circumcised, and did not conform to the rites of the Mosaic law, he was still in doubts whether his prayers were heard, or his alms accepted as evidences of his faith and piety. The angel's words were, therefore, peculiarly fit words for Cornelius. And they, moreover, contain a great truth as to the divine method of dealing with mankind: that God prefers the offering of the heart to external forms, however imposing or ceremonious, however pompous and costly. God requireth not so much sacrifice, nor whole burnt offerings, but obedience.

And now send men to Joppa—a seaport town distant about thirty-five miles, the nearest port to Jerusalem on the Mediterranean. This is doubtless one of the oldest towns in the world. Its origin is lost in the twilight of time. Its antiquity is lost in a mass of classic fables. Pliny asserts that it existed before the Deluge. Many Greek and Jewish traditions may be found that ascribe its foundation to Noah, and say that he built the ark here. We know at least that it was a city at the conquest of Joshua. To this port Hiram, King of Tyre, sent the lumber from the mountains of Lebanon for the building of Solomon's temple, and from hence it was carried up by animals to the holy city. This city is mentioned in the history of the Asmonean princes; but is referred to in the New Testament only in connection with Peter's visit. Here he raised Tabitha from the dead, and was lodging when the centurion sent for him. We have found Jonah, the old Hebrew missionary to Nineveh, taking ship at this port to flee from the Lord. In the Crusades, and in Napoleon's Syrian wars, Joppa was a place of importance. It is still a town of about 5,000 inhabitants, one-fourth of whom are reckoned to be Christians.

And call for one Simon, whose surname is Peter: he lodgeth with one Simon, a tanner. Our word tanner comes from *tanit*, cognate with French *teindre*, to stain. The Greek word used here is *burseus*, which means a *skinner*—that is, of animals; and here used in the sense of a skin-softener, a leather-maker, *a tanner*. This occupation was not highly esteemed by the ancients. Simon was probably one of the early converts to Christianity. In ancient times tanners used have their houses and workshops, as is common with us, out of the city, or apart from the main crowded thoroughfares, on account of the fetid odor arising from the dead animals and raw hides, and *near rivers* for the convenience of water. *At Joppa* may mean no more than that he was near to it, or in the suburbs. The Hebrew *Mishna* required all such employments to be carried on at some distance from the towns.

In Europe and the East it is common to give a specific address to every letter, and to describe in all legal documents a man's rank, occupation or profession. A. B. is a gentleman. C. D. is a barrister at law. E. F. is a medical man. G. H. is a weaver, a farmer, a machinist, or a *currier* or *tanner*. And so in passports from one government to another. *Simon a tanner* is designated. He resides there and is known. Peter was only there on a visit, and his profession was not known, at least not among the people. If Cornelius had sent for Peter *the Pope*, he would not have found him even to this day, or even for Peter *the Apostle*, he would not have found him. His messengers, however, did find Simon a tanner, and Simon Peter upon his housetop engaged in prayer. Observe all these characters are remarkable for prayer and for visions. Cornelius prays, and has a vision to send for Peter. Peter is praying when the messengers arrive, and falling into a trance, has a vision by which he is convinced that he ought to go with them. Peter's host was a poor man; he probably had no prophet's chamber; no upper room for his accommodation. It was common, however, in that country, for the people to retire to their housetops for meditation, rest or prayer. This custom is often alluded to in the Bible. The tops of the houses in the East are flat. A traveller may now go almost all over the city of Cairo, Damascus, or Jerusalem, on the roofs of houses, without ever descending to the streets.

He fell into a trance. Verse 10. Greek is, there fell on him an ecstasy, which seems to mean a preternatural state of mind, which was intended to prepare him for the vision. In this kind of a trance the mind seems to retire from the body, and to be wholly absorbed with spiritual or internal objects; a rapture of soul giving the face a look of astonishment, and rendering the subject for the time insensible to external objects, or to anything else than the subject then occupying the soul. The books mention many extraordinary cases, which it is impossible fully to understand or explain with our present knowledge of the connection that subsists between the mind and the external world, the soul and the body. The whole subject of the connection of the mind and the body is yet to be studied. I should not wonder if we are on the eve of great discoveries in religious psychology.

Please read here *verses 9 to 33, inclusive.* Observe their address and skill in opening their errand to Peter. *And they said, Cornelius the centurion, a just man, and one that feareth God, and of good report among all the nations of the Jews, was warned from God by an holy angel to send for thee into his house, and to hear words of thee.* This is one of the most happily conceived and successfully applied addresses in the world. They admit at once that their master is a Roman officer, but to remove the prejudices which might be in Peter's mind as a Jew against him, they say, although he is a centurion, he is *a just man*—though an officer in the Roman army that has conquered and still holds your country in subjection, he is a man of integrity and courtesy, and he *fears God* and worships the one living and true God of the Jews; he is not a cruel, savage idolater; and he has an excellent reputation among your own countrymen; and God has sent his holy angel to tell him to send for thee; and to send for thee to come into his house, to hear words of thee. The point made was very strong. God had shown so much regard for Cornelius as to send an holy angel from heaven to tell him to send for Peter, and to tell Peter that he must go to the Roman officer's quarters, and there preach to him about Jesus. The message was from heaven. Peter was certainly called of God to go to Cesarea. And remembering Peter's vision on the housetop, we are not surprised that in spite of his prejudices, he was convinced and went.

Then called he them in, and lodged them. And on the morrow Peter went away with them, and certain brethren from Joppa accompanied them.

As a matter of respect to Peter, Cornelius had sent two of his household, and a devout soldier as a guard. The roads were not free from robbers. In the East a person seldom travels alone. They are from habit, if not from necessity, a gregarious people. They live in villages. Their transactions and journeys are always made in companies. It will frequently happen, if you ask a man why he came to the place where you find him, he will point to an other man who seems to be the greater business man, and say, I came because he did. In the East, if a man go to a court of justice, he is followed by as many of his acquaintances as possible, who canvass all the probabilities of his case, and have a salvo for every exigency, and a *salaam* for every one they dare to hope they can influence in his behalf. They are warm-tempered and social in their habits, and then it is always necessary to have witnesses to all and everything that is said and done. This custom explains the importance attached in the Bible to the company a man keeps, and the solemn warnings given against evil companions. Nor are these warnings any the less important now and among us. One sinner destroyeth much good. The companion of fools shall be destroyed.

Certain brethren went with Peter. How many we do not know. Perhaps six. It was respectful to Cornelius for Peter to have some friends with him. His companions were no doubt also, at least in part, acquainted with his trance and vision. And as he was going on a new and difficult mission, they went with him to comfort him, and be witnesses of what should befall him, or of what he should do. And surely it was a gracious Providence that moved them to go with him. It was desirable they should be witnesses of his reception by Cornelius, and of his preaching, and of the grace of God shown to the centurion; and be able to testify of these things when Peter should be called to an account by his countrymen for having gone among the Gentiles. And now, before we enter upon the consideration of Peter's sermon, let us gather up some reflections from the history. And

First. As Peter stands before us, we have an admirable example of piety, zeal and faithfulness. He is engaged in his proper mission at Joppa—earnestly praying when he falls into a trance, receives a vision from heaven, and is prepared to understand the messengers of Cornelius, who were then just arrived in Joppa. And when he reached Cesarea, and Cornelius tells him all that he had done, and all that had been told to him, and says to him: "And thou hast well done that thou art come. Now, therefore, are we all here present before God, to hear all things that are commanded thee of God; then Peter opened his mouth and said—preaching peace by Jesus Christ," etc. Peter was far from being sinless, but he was a man of prayer and of earnest simplicity. Like David, he prayed and called upon God evening and morning; and as more is given to him that hath, that is, to him that uses aright what he has, so we find the enlightening, converting process carried on in Peter's mind until he has overcome his narrow prejudices against the Gentiles, and with a clear conscience opens to them the kingdom of Christ. That which at first he could not at all apprehend—which was dark and unaccountable—is made plain. And just so it was with the Roman officer. He is diligent in the use of the best means and of all the light he has, and then more is given to him. In proportion as we are willing to know the truth, and seek for it with an honest heart as for hidden treasure, in the same proportion we shall find it and be sanctified by it. It is by the truth we are to be made free from the bondage of error and the tyranny of Satan. If any man, says our Lord, will *do* the will of God he shall know of the doctrine, whether it be of God or not.

Second. We have here a beautiful union of personal and relative duties. This Roman officer "feared God with all his house." So did Abraham, and for it he received special divine commendation, and so did Joshua and Lydia. There is nothing more important to the well-being of cities and states than family religion. The purity and intelligence of our families lie at the very foundation of our social and civil prosperity. The elements of our strength are in our families. One of the greatest causes of social degradation and political insubordination is the want of family religion and instruction. Public schools, Sunday schools, and the press and the pulpit are powerless without the co-operation of parents. The fountains that flow over the land, covering it in all its length and breadth, rise in our households and receive their qualities of good or evil chiefly where they first break forth. Parents are teachers by their example; but this is not enough. They must do as well as teach. They must govern, restrain and instruct. Every parent is called upon by all the love he has for his child and for his country, and as he values his soul, to say like Joshua, "as for me and my house, we will serve the Lord."

"They who rock the cradle rule the world."

Third. We have here the union of piety and morality. Cornelius gave alms to all the people, and he prayed to God always. Piety and morality are both blessed realities, but they must not be confounded. A pious man must be a moral man, but a man may be respectable in his morals who is not pious. A man may reform himself from bad habits because he finds they are injurious to his reputation and his health. And this is well, and in so far he is to be commended; but before he can claim to be pious, he must fear God and pray to Him, and put his trust for salvation in the Lord Jesus Christ as He is offered in the

Gospel. Piety is a living reality—a beauty that is "a joy forever." It is more than the forms of a ritual. It is a dynamic power that permeates the whole man from the heart outward. But as fatal errors are common on this subject, let us look at it for a few moments. Some seem to think they must be Christians, and talk of their communion with God, who are cruel, hard-hearted, close-handed and unjust. But this cannot be so. They are deceived. God never joined such things together. "Whoso," saith an apostle, "hath this world's goods, and seeth his brother have need, and shutteth up his bowels of compassion from him, how dwelleth the love of God in him?" Others are amiable and well to do in the world, and have a fair reputation with their fellow-men, but they live without God. Their Maker is not in all their thoughts. They have no love for Jesus Christ. They are dead in trespasses and in sins. Indulging their sensual passions, they vainly hope, by a few gifts of charity, to cover a multitude of sins. But what saith the Bible on this very matter? "Pure religion and undefiled before God and the Father is this, to visit the fatherless and widows in their affliction, and to keep themselves unspotted from the world." *James.*

Fourth. Here also we have a union of *reality* with *eminence* in the true religion. "He gave *much* alms to the people, and prayed to God *always*." Now, there cannot be eminence in grace without reality; but there may be a reality where there is not eminence. But as Christians, it is our duty to grow in grace and in the knowledge of our Lord Jesus Christ, adding the excellences of religion to its essentials. We should have life, and have it more abundantly. Our hearts should be enlarged. We should seek to be filled with all the fullness of God.

It were, however, wholly to misconstrue this portion of the Word of God, and to contradict the teaching of all the apostles, if we were to conclude that Cornelius was accepted of God on account of his morality and alms. We can be justified only by faith—not by works. We are saved by grace—not by our own merits.

It is, therefore, a palpable abuse of this history to make it a plea for trusting in our own righteousness—for trusting in our own morality and culture—as if the having of such things justified a man for rejecting Christ. This did not the centurion. He feared God, worshipped him, prayed to God always, and gave alms to the people; and just as soon as he heard of Jesus Christ, he believed in him and was baptized, professing his full conversion to him. He was ready to receive salvation by the Gospel, notwithstanding his good works. He was an honest, earnest man—humble and teachable as a child. And in all these particulars he differs widely from the self-righteous of our day. They are full of cavils and technicalities—self-confident and wiser than their teachers. They boast of their decency and refinement, their love of the fine arts and of poetry, and are good enough to be saved without Christ. Now the Roman centurion was as good a man by nature, and by practice, and by self-culture, to say the least, as any of these self-righteous Pharisees, and probably much better, and yet he did not think it enough to be moral and respectable. He did not rest satisfied with such things. He continues to pray to God for more light and grace, and God hears him, and as soon as he is told what to do, he obeys. He sends to Joppa, and when Peter arrives, says, now we are all here before God to hear words from thee as to what we must do to be saved—all things that God shall command thee to say unto us. And when Peter explains to him who Jesus is, and that it is the Divine method of salvation that all men, Jew and Gentile, must believe in the Son of God and confess him with the mouth unto salvation, then Cornelius and his household were obedient—believed and were baptized. The moral and decent and respectable men, therefore, instead of being justified by the centurion's case for not believing in Christ and professing faith in him is condemned—most strongly condemned by him.

Nor is there ever any controversy between good morals and the Gospel. The alms and prayers of the centurion were a memorial in his behalf before God. And it is true that all due honor is given to him for his piety and good works, heathen though he was or had been—for he was not yet circumcised, nor up to this time does he seem to have known anything about believing in Jesus as the Messiah. But surely God is not straitened for means by which to reach the human heart. He called Abram out of Ur of the Chaldees. And Job in the land of Uz was a pious man. Melchizedek was a pious king amid heathen neighbors. And here we find Cornelius, a Roman officer—*a devout man and one that feared God.* And so in all lands and cities some are prepared to receive the Gospel as soon as it is preached.

But it is not said that Cornelius was accepted of God for his mere morality. Nor does it appear that he himself ever thought of depending upon it. From the history the very reverse would appear as true. His heart was evidently touched. He did not trust to his alms, nor to his forms of prayer; but was *devout*—sincere and fervent in his worship of God according to the best light he had. Is it not an abuse, then, for any man to argue that as Cornelius was a good man *before* he heard of the Gospel, that he may be a good man who hears it and *rejects* it? This Cornelius did not do. He was a devout man according to all that he knew, and was ready to receive the Gospel as soon as he heard it. The case, then, is a very different one from that of a man who depends upon his mere external morality in a Christian land as a substitute for Christianity. Cornelius was found in the way of obedience to all known duty. Not content with his prayers and alms, he is seeking to know and to do more, and as soon and as far as he is instructed, we see him acting promptly. But where is the man among us who boasts of his fashionable morality that does this? Cornelius is diligent in all the forms of religion that he knew how to use, and maintains them successfully in his family, and then gladly embraces Jesus Christ as his Saviour as soon as he is preached to him. This the man among us, who thinks himself good enough to be saved without a Saviour, does not do. He improved the light he had, and more was given unto him. His good works show that he was under divine influence even when he was ignorant whence it came. He was a subject of free and sovereign grace, and as soon as Jesus is preached to him, he accepts of Him as a Saviour. The man, therefore, among us who attempts to justify his neglect of the Gospel by the case of Cornelius, only condemns himself. And as Cornelius was not a vain, self-righteous man, so neither was he an antinomian. He was no fatalist. His religion was a working religion. Without knowing anything of Paul, or of his preaching or epistles, he was obeying, with all his might, the injunction given to the *Philippians:* Work out your own salvation with fear and trembling, for it is God that worketh in you both to will and to do of his good pleasure.

Finally, this history illustrates the universality of the Gospel dispensation. We have recently found that a Hebrew missionary (Jonah) was sent from Joppa, in a way that he did not choose, to preach to the Ninevites; and here we find Peter sent from the same place to open up the kingdom of God to the Gentiles. By an extraordinary vision he is convinced that the high wall between the Jews and the Gentiles was broken down.

The Jewish idea that a man was to be saved certainly and simply because he was born a Jew is no longer to prevail. It never was correct. God does not save any man because of his birth, rank, talents or external privileges. Nor does God exclude any man from his favor on account of these things.

The New Testament shows most clearly that in the matter of salvation, there is no difference between Jew and Gentile, bond and free. God is no respecter of persons. He will not save a man because he is a Jew or because he is an Anglo-Saxon. Nor will he condemn him simply because he is a Chinese or a Walla-Walla Digger. The whole human race lie before God upon the same level—stand on the same platform. None are to be saved merely on account of external privileges—none are to be lost simply or merely for the want of them. All are guilty. All have come short of the glory of God. If any are saved, it must be owing to God's sovereign mercy. And now it hath pleased him that all men everywhere should believe the Gospel, repent and be saved. "But in every nation, he that feareth him and worketh righteousness, is accepted with him." "The sacrifices of God are a broken spirit: a broken and a contrite heart, O God, thou wilt not despise."

VIII.

THE CENTURION OF CESAREA CONTINUED.

3.—*Peter's Sermon on the Occasion of his Conversion.*

Then Peter opened his mouth, and said, Of a truth I perceive that God is no respecter of persons: But in every nation he that feareth him, and worketh righteousness, is accepted with him. The word which God sent unto the children of Israel, preaching peace by Jesus Christ: (he is Lord of all:) That word (I say), ye know, which was published throughout all Judea, and began from Galilee, after the baptism which John preached; How God anointed Jesus of Nazareth with the Holy Ghost and with power: who went about doing good, and healing all that were oppressed of the devil; for God was with him. And we are witnesses of all things which he did both in the land of the Jews, and in Jerusalem; whom they slew and hanged on a tree: Him God raised up the third day and showed him openly: Not to all the people, but unto witnesses chosen before of God, even to us, who did eat and drink with him after he rose from the dead. And he commanded us to preach unto the people, and to testify that it is he which was ordained of God to be the Judge of quick and dead. To him give all the prophets witness, that through his name whosoever believeth in him shall receive remission of sins.

While Peter yet spake these words, the Holy Ghost fell on all them which heard the word. And they of the circumcision which believed were astonished, as many as came with Peter, because that on the Gentiles also was poured out the gift of the Holy Ghost. For they heard them speak with tongues, and magnify God. Then answered Peter: Can any man forbid water, that these should not be baptized, which have received the Holy Ghost as well as we? And he commanded them to be baptized in the name of the Lord. Then prayed they him to tarry certain days.—*Acts* x. 34 *to end of chapter.*

This chapter contains an account of the reception of Gentile converts into the Gospel church without the intermediate state of Judaism. The introduction to the conversion of Cornelius (chap. ix. 31–43, and chap. xi. 1–18) is the appendix. The whole history is one of great interest to us. The main facts in regard to this distinguished convert are, his country, his profession, rank and residence, and that we are to regard him as the representative man of all Gentile nations; the first who was received into the Gospel Church after the day of Pentecost, and without passing through the gate of proselytism to Judaism. This interesting subject of converting grace we have found where we should not antecedently have looked for such a history; we have found a pious heathen, a Roman officer, who was devout, feared God, gave alms to all the people, and prayed always. We have, therefore, found the church of the living God in the Roman army, in the service of a Pagan emperor. And in looking for the means employed for producing such a result, we discover them to have been ordinary and supernatural; the light of nature, the strength of the natural conscience, the force of tradition and the direct illumination of the Spirit of almighty grace. And for the purpose of making known to this distinguished man the way of salvation through Jesus Christ, we have seen that he has a vision, and an angel of God is sent to tell him to send for Peter. Accordingly the centurion's messengers travel some thirty-five or forty miles from Cesarea to Joppa, and find Peter lodging with one Simon, a tanner, and when he is convinced that it is his duty to go and preach Jesus among the Gentiles, and even to a Roman centurion, he lodges the messengers with him till morning, and then goes with them to Cesarea. Olshausen concludes Cornelius was not a proselyte to the Hebrew religion, but was in the process of becoming one. Perhaps already so far advanced as to be "a proselyte of the gate." But the whole force and meaning of the narrative is, we think, lost, if Cornelius had embraced Judaism. The description given of him is not that of a proselyte, "in any technical or formal sense, but of a Gentile whom divine grace had prepared for the immediate reception of the Gospel, without passing through the intermediate state of Judaism, although long familiar with it, and indebted to it for such knowledge of the word of God as he possessed." *Prof. J. A. Alexander in loco.* But in calling Cornelius *a pious heathen* we are not to be understood to mean that he was saved without or independent of Jesus Christ. Peter declares that his case proved that whoever in every nation feareth God and worketh righteousness, is accepted of him. Righteousness toward our fellow-men, and piety toward God, must indeed go together. But no man is justified in the sight of God, except through the mediation of Jesus Christ. But infants, idiots, and such heathen as Cornelius, who have no knowledge of the Son of God, or are incapable of knowing who he is, may nevertheless receive the grace of God for his sake and be saved through him. It is the opinion of Owen, one of the ablest Biblical interpreters and one of our greatest theologians, that the angels who have kept their first estate, are confirmed in glory by the death of Christ. It is on this ground that we hope for the salvation of Socrates. For while no one is saved independent of Christ, such as we have named may be saved by him without being aware of it till their salvation is completed. The character and previous history of Cornelius are therefore worthy of special attention. He was *a devout man*, pious not merely in a heathen sense, but *feared God*, the one only living and true God. He was diligent in keeping the seven precepts of Noah, which forbade idolatry, profanity, incest, murder, dishonesty, the eating of blood or of anything strangled, and required all murderers to be put to death. This was the sum of the religion of the whole world, until heathenism began to prevail, and then it was still the religion of the Patriarchs, from Abraham to Moses.

It is plain from the Old Testament that some recognition of JEHOVAH as the God of the Hebrews, was common among the surrounding nations, and not inconsistent with their polytheism; but Cornelius had abandoned all false gods and all idolatry, and feared the true God in opposition to the gods of heathendom. And he taught all his family to do the same. He feared God *with all his house.* His religion was also a living reality, for he abounded in charities, and was punctual and spiritual in his prayers, asking wisdom from God to direct him in all things. Now in the bringing of this man into the Church, we see how divine providence arranges the means and provides the agents for performing the parts assigned to them. The providential means used for the centurion's conversion were twofold, a vision to himself and a trance and a vision to Peter. The first was to assure Cornelius that God had a perfect knowledge of his ways, and designed to show him mercy, and direct him what to do in order that he might be saved. The other vision to Peter was intended to convince him that the old high partition wall between Jews and Gentiles was now broken down, and that he should, therefore, meet the advances of Cornelius though he was a Roman centurion. It was a kind providence that took Peter to Joppa and detained him there, for Joppa was easy of access from Cesarea. And it was a gracious providence that overruled the time and the manner of the two visions, and that furnished Cornelius suitable men for his message to Joppa. The divine regard for Cornelius is seen moreover in sending an angel to him, and in giving Peter so instructive and impressive a vision. The sheet let down to him, the *Thone*, was emblematical of the extending of the Gospel to all men, and its *four corners* knit together aptly typical of the four quarters of the globe, south, east, north and west, that are embraced in the Gospel offer. As there was an earnest and worthy purpose in the vision to Cornelius—the vision was not designed to amuse, frighten, or astonish him, but to direct him how to proceed in order that he might know his whole duty—so also, the details of

Peter's vision, and the story of the men from Joppa, and their account of God's manifestation to their master, and the enlightening of his mind at the time by the Spirit of God, all concurred in preparing the Roman officer to meet Peter, and in preparing Peter also to meet him. A blessed Providence was working all the time with both of them, though at first they knew it not. How wonderful and gracious was the chain of providence that brought about the conversion of Cornelius! A vision to him and a trance upon Peter—wonderful coincidences preparing the way for the opening of the door of Christ's kingdom to the Gentiles! But God is no less wonderful and gracious now than he was then. He is full of compassion. He knows all our trials and temptations. He knoweth our frame and remembereth that we are but dust. How often do we overrate ourselves and underrate God's mercies! His grace is always sufficient. To him be all the glory.

Beginning at Galilee. Verse 37. Please read here from verse 34 to the end of the chapter. According to Peter and the evangelists, the order of our Lord's manifestations is on this wise: He was baptized by John, then goes into the desert and remains forty days, then returns to John the Baptist, who was at Bethany or Bethabara, and made disciples of Andrew, Bartholomew, Peter and Philip, and went afterward to Capernaum and wrought many miracles in Galilee. These things had been a long time so notorious, that Peter presumes Cornelius to be acquainted with them.

First. PETER'S SERMON before the centurion shows that he was now able to understand the natural theology of human races. *God is no respecter of persons*—that is, the divine favor is not, as we have heretofore taught, confined to Israelites—a pious Gentile, a man who, like Cornelius, fears God, is accepted in his sight, though he has not the same form of worship that the Jews have, or that we Christians have. A wicked man is not accepted of God on account of his external advantages. His race and wealth and honors and forms of religion may all be proper in their place, but it is not *for* them that he is to be saved. The divine rule is to regard the heart and proceed with men according to their true and real character. It was a fatal mistake, therefore, for his countrymen to think that they could not be lost, however wicked they might be, because they were descended from Abraham; and that a Gentile could not be saved, however pious his manner of life might be, simply because he was born a Gentile. God is a sovereign, and bestows his gifts, both temporal and spiritual, after his own will and pleasure. Peter's vision presented in the same sheet, animals clean and unclean; that is, such as were used in Hebrew sacrifices and such as were forbidden according to the ceremonial law. And the force of this vision is also the more clearly apprehended when we remember that unclean animals were considered by the Jews as an image of the Gentiles. In the book of the Revelation of St. John, *four beasts* and *four and twenty elders* are supposed to represent the Gentile and Jewish churches; that is, converts from among the heathen and the Jews. "What God hath cleansed that call not thou common or unclean."

Bengel has very happily remarked here that it is not an indifferentism of religions, but an indifferency; that is, an impartiality as to the acceptance of nations that is spoken of. Peter does not say as some of the *savans* of our day do, that all religions are equally good, but that whoever is truly and practically pious in every nation God accepts without any partiality as to their nationality. "Peter is not here denying a sovereign and discriminating choice, but one founded on mere national distinctions. I now at length understand that although God bestows his favors as he will, he does not mean to limit them hereafter as of old to any one race of people." *Alexander*. But was not this always true? Most certainly. It was true from the beginning, that whoever feared God and wrought righteousness was accepted of him. But Peter had not perceived it before; the fault, however, was his own. And his discovery of the truth now was not owing to his superior learning or intellectual investigation, but to God's revelations to him. Nor does his discovery add anything to the store of sovereign grace. It is not more true in itself now than before; but his eyes are opened to see what he had not been able to see. Even as long ago as Cain's transgression, we find the Almighty remonstrating with him as to his unreasonable views of sin and his moral condition." "If thou doest well, shalt thou not be accepted? If not well, sin and its punishment lieth at thy door." *Gen.* iv. 7. It had always been true that the kingdom of God consisted not in meat and drink, but in righteousness, joy and peace in the Holy Ghost. But now this truth is made more manifest. Now it is clearly seen that in Christ Jesus there is neither circumcision nor uncircumcision, but a new heart—a new creature. The inquiry at the last day will not be as to what nation or country we belonged to, nor whether we were baptized in this church or in some other, but how have we *felt* and *acted* toward God and our fellow men? Our conduct, our faith and actions toward God and man will be the subjects examined into at the judgment of Almighty God.

Second. Peter's sermon was an original dis

course—a new one. It contained truths as old as the creation, but not known to him or to his hearers before. Columbus' discovery of America did not create the continent, nor did Newton's discoveries in astronomy call the heavenly bodies into existence. Peter's preaching was new only in the sense of apprehending and explaining the will of God, which on these points he had not before understood. And hence we find his discourse historical, doctrinal, expository, and practical. And although the Gentiles who lived among or near the Jews were more or less acquainted with their religion, and the histories of their Scriptures, they knew little if anything at all about the character, life, doctrines, preaching and precepts or true claims of Jesus as the Messiah, until they were especially instructed by the preaching of the apostles.

That word, ye know, which was published throughout all the land of Judea—that is, a report of Jesus and his miracles was well known among the people, even from the baptism and preaching of John. "And of all that I now preach, we are witnesses of all things which he did both in the land of the Jews and in Jerusalem, whom they slew and hanged on a tree; Him God raised up the third day, and shewed him openly not to all the people, but unto witnesses chosen before of God." *Verses* 39-41.

Not to all the people. Why not? 1. Because the times were sadly out of joint; suspicious and seditious. It would have caused commotion or trouble. Some would have cried this is he, and others have said, it is like him; and others would have denied everything in the confusion, and the validity of the testimony would have been weakened rather than established. 2. The right kind of witnesses were chosen of God, namely: such as knew him intimately, had known him a long time, and who had nothing to gain by giving false testimony. It was impossible for them to have been mistaken, or to find a reasonable motive for them to deceive others, nor was their testimony ever successfully impeached. They were his daily companions for more than three years before the crucifixion, and "they did eat and drink with him after he rose from the dead." They saw the prints of the nails and the gash of the spear, and they saw him ascend into heaven, and if this was not true, why did not their enemies produce his body? 3. The testimony of these eye witnesses was as perfect as if Jesus had been shown to great multitudes. In the law the testimony of two or three is as good as a hundred. One demonstration in mathematics is as conclusive as a thousand. The witnesses were sufficient in number. They were in every way competent. Their knowledge was accurate. Their veracity above reasonable suspicion. Their motives absolutely unquestionable. And then, after all, our conviction of the truth of all these things must rest upon testimony. Before our conversion, we have no proof of the truth of religion but upon testimony. We do not know anything that we have not seen or felt ourselves, except from the testimony of others. We are shut up to the necessity of receiving conviction by faith. Society is a rope of sand without a reliance upon human testimony. We cannot live without it.

And even if Jesus had been shown with all

the marks of his crucifixion palpable to every man, woman, and child in the Hebrew nation, still *we* must believe upon testimony, and the testimony we have is as strong as human witnesses can make it. Peter, therefore, shows that the resurrection of Jesus was a proof of his Messiahship, and appeals to it as a fact then publicly known, at least to a sufficient number of the most competent witnesses—witnesses chosen before of God to bear this testimony, and in order that they might do so understandingly, they were intimately acquainted with him before his death, and they were with him repeatedly and in a great many different places, and at many different times after his resurrection; and had a great deal of free conversation with him, "who did eat and drink with him after he rose from the dead." It was impossible for them to be deceived. Nor was there any motive for them to deceive others.

Third. The *forty-third* verse is the conclusion of Peter's sermon. "To Him give all the prophets witness, that through his name, whosoever believeth in him, shall receive remission of sins."

As if the preacher had said, Our testimony is indeed that of honest, competent witnesses, and about things that have recently taken place, and concerning which if we have not told the truth, we can soon be exposed; but our testimony is also confirmed by all the prophets, and they all come to the same conclusion, namely: that whosoever believeth in Jesus of Nazareth shall receive remission of sins, for their testimony proves him to be the anointed of God, the long-promised Messiah. Like the prophets and apostles, ministers of the Gospel then are to preach to the people concerning Christ. They are his ambassadors, and should themselves be witnesses of his power to save. The subject matter of their preaching is the remission of sins through faith in his name. That is, that the forgiveness of sin is to be obtained for his sake; that therefore all men are sinners; that there is need for the atonement; that it is a faithful saying and worthy of all acceptation that Jesus Christ came into the world to save sinners, even the chief of sinners; and that the great need of all men is the remission of their sins, and holiness, without which they cannot see God in peace. By the taking away—"the remission of sins"—Peter means the removing of their guilt, power, nature and consequences. And this implies their pardon and our acceptance with God, reconciliation to Him, sanctification and complete redemption—A GLORIOUS SALVATION. The apostle is careful to speak of the dignity of our Lord. He is the anointed of God; and yet He was diligent in his work, and died for our redemption. He also reminds Cornelius that the Gospel which he was then hearing was venerable for its antiquity. It has always been the true and only religion for man as a sinner.

Fourth. THE RESULTS OF PETER'S SERMON. "The Holy Ghost fell on them which heard the word." *Verse* 44, etc.

1. The Holy Ghost, then, is something distinct and separate from the Word; and yet is necessary to make the Word effectual, even when spoken by an inspired man. The Spirit of inspiration was on Peter, and while by it he was speaking, the Spirit fell on his hearers.

Thus was God honored in his Word, and thus did he honor the word and ministry of his servant.

2. The Holy Ghost fell upon these Gentiles *before* they were baptized. So Abraham was justified by faith before he was circumcised. Cornelius and his friends, while yet Peter is preaching, received the Holy Ghost. This proves that baptismal regeneration is not according to the Gospel. Here was the baptism of the Holy Ghost before and wholly independent of the baptism with water that was subsequently administered. And here also we have a plain proof that God is not confined to any set of ordinances or external signs. The Holy Ghost was no respecter of modes. The flesh profiteth nothing. It is the Spirit that quickeneth.

3. But it certainly is an error to say that water baptism is unnecessary to those who have received the baptism of the Holy Spirit, for the very reason given for baptizing them with water is that they have been baptized with the Spirit. It is enough for us to know

that baptism with water is a sacrament appointed by our Lord, and that he has made it the door of admission into his visible church, and a seal of the new covenant. Though the Holy One of Israel is not limited in his works, nor fettered by ordinances as we are, yet we have no right to presume on his grace in any other than in his own appointed ways. We are not to trust in, nor neglect the ordinances of religion. They are divinely appointed channels of grace and salvation, and yet they do not of themselves convey essential grace; but lead to Christ who is all in all.

4. *Can any man forbid water?* clearly means —who can forbid that water should be brought in? There is no probability—scarcely, indeed, is it possible—that there was any immersion in this case. There was no preparation for such a mode of baptism. The Roman centurion was not likely to have had a baptistery or baptismal font in his quarters. And if he had, and they were going to it, then the form of the expression would have been: Who can forbid us *to go to the water?* The distinction between ap-

plying the subject for baptism *to* the water, or applying the water *to* the subject, is important, for it goes very far toward settling the question about the mode of baptism. And surely in this case the water was applied *to* Cornelius, and not Cornelius *to* the water, and it was applied by pouring or sprinkling. "Can any man forbid water"—however rigid a Jew he may be—however ceremonious he may be—can he forbid water, " that these should not be baptized, who have received the Holy Ghost as well as we?" The argument is perfectly conclusive. "What God hath cleansed, that call not thou common or unclean." Shall we deny the *sign* to those who have received from God himself the thing signified? Are not those on whom God has bestowed the grace of the covenant plainly entitled to the seals of that covenant? Surely we should follow God's example, and receive those into our communion whom he hath taken into fellowship with himself by giving them his Holy Spirit. This rule, applied to the subjects and mode of baptism, and also to the order of ministers and mode of their consecration and worship, would teach us to be liberal in our views, and to love all who love our Lord Jesus Christ.

A few points of Christian character and of practical divinity developed in this history of the conversion of Cornelius, are worthy of a distinct notification.

1. One cannot but observe it as a remarkable feature in apostolic character, that they were *self-denying* and *disinterested* in their labors. After the day of Pentecost, where and when do we find them wanting in courage, or showing any *symptoms of selfishness?* Never do we find them pursuing schemes of ambition or of worldly glory. They were so intent on the glory of their Master and the salvation of the souls of men that they were themselves content to be forgotten and overlooked. They were never tired *of*, though sometimes weary *in*, the service of God.

2. *In the conversion of a Roman centurion we have a proof of the power of the Gospel as well as of its expansiveness.*

It is strange the apostles should have con

ceived that the command to go and disciple all nations, meant only such nations or persons as had embraced the Jewish religion; yet this was their idea at first, and it was very difficult to remove it. But here we have an illustration of God's method of honoring his word, the preaching of which he has made the great instrument or means of converting and saving men. Cornelius was not taught what to do by any direct illumination. Nor was the angel employed himself to preach the Gospel, but to introduce the preacher—to tell Cornelius where to find Peter, who should tell him what to do. This is a striking demonstration that it is God's will for every one to do just what he is told to do, and also of the worth of combining human and divine agency in the work of Christianizing the world. It was as easy for the angel to have told Cornelius of Jesus as to tell him of Peter. But the divine purpose was to bring Peter and Cornelius together—a Jew and a Gentile. The supernatural messages to Peter all carried their great lesson with them, until Peter is prepared to go to a Gentile. God thus opened up Peter's heart to the largeness and liberality of the Gospel economy, and prepared the way for him to meet Cornelius, and in the meantime Cornelius has been so prepared, that when he is brought into personal contact with Peter, his mind is opened, and Peter's words convey life and power to him. We must not forget that this was done by divine aid. The Holy Ghost fell on them. God hath joined means and ends together. God's works of creation and providence, and also of grace, are all wonderful. They all display his wisdom, power and goodness. In Cornelius we see that the Holy One of Israel is not limited. Oracles are good, but no mere outward rites of religion are sufficient. They are helps. They are not to be despised or treated with neglect, neither are we to trust in them. To what extent God operates on the minds of individual heathens we know not. A remarkable case is recorded of the Flathead Indians of the Rocky Mountains, who sent a deputation of four to St. Louis, in the days of General Clarke, to know what was taught in the white man's Bible.

Speaking with reverence, it was just as easy for God to have commanded the angel to tell Cornelius what to do, as to tell him to instruct Cornelius to send to Joppa for Peter. This would have saved the centurion a great deal of trouble and time; but this was not God's method. The means appointed for the conversion of the world must be honored. The treasure is indeed in earthen vessels, that the excellency of the power may be of God and not of man. It hath pleased God by the foolishness of preaching to save them that believe. Angels may be employed in carrying messages of love to other worlds. They have summoned some of our own race in past ages, to listen to the glad tidings of free grace; but God's great plan is to convert men chiefly by the preaching of the Gospel by men of *like passions with ourselves*—men who are converted and called to the work by the Holy Spirit; who can sympathize with us, and tell us from their own experience what religion is, and how sinners are to be saved.

3. In admiring the excellent character of Cornelius, we must be careful to distinguish be-

tween the *procuring* cause of his salvation and the evidences of his piety. And we must avoid, as we have already said in the former discourses, confounding his *morality* with his *piety*, or substituting his alms and prayers for his acceptance of Christ when preached to him. Exemplary and amiable and sincere in his bearing as a man and as a soldier, his morality led him to Christ. He did not think of depending on it and of rejecting Christ because of it. His piety was personal, earnest, social and domestic, as if he had been trained in the camp of that heroic general and prince, who said most firmly before an assembled nation : "As for me," even if you are faithless, "as for me and my house, we will serve the Lord." His piety and works of righteousness were accepted of God, but did not merit divine grace. And so now we must use the means of grace, for although they do not of themselves save, yet we have no right to expect salvation without them.

4. Nor should we forget to observe the *moral* courage of this Roman. He breaks away first from the idols he was taught to worship

in his youth, and adopts the religion of Noah; and then he has the courage to own his change of religion and to practise its holy precepts. And this he does in the face, *first*, of the contempt which all the world had for the Jews, and especially for their religion; and *secondly*, in opposition to the law of the empire that forbade any Roman citizen to receive any strange or new religion. But he was obedient to the heavenly vision and sent for Peter, and then heard his preaching, and submitted to the terms of admission into the Christian Church. He was baptized and became a member of Christ's Church. And it may be, that it is just here many of my hearers fail. They have knowledge. It may be they are even learned; but they have not moral courage. Without some touch of the heroic spirit, there is not much that is great or good effected in our world. In every department of life, it seems to us the great want of our times is *courage to do right*. In business, there are so many temptations to do wrong, that a man of a weak and vacillating temper is almost sure to go astray. And in the religious enterprises of the day, there is need not only of an honest heart, but of a courage and a resolution that will shrink from no toil or weariness. That religion is very weak that evaporates in sentiment. Knowledge is worth but little that is not applied. Elegant culture is a graceful ornament, but it does not renew the heart. It is but as the pale moonbeams on the waves, that can do nothing to stop their raging. *What our age wants is moral courage*—high moral integrity united to a heart that knows no fear. And yet it is much more rare to find a man of true moral courage than to find one of amiable qualities, or of learning. There are thousands who

> ———" See the good, and approve it too,
> Abhor the wrong, and yet the wrong pursue,"

because they have not firmness of principle, nor courage to make a stand against the wrong. We find Joseph of Arimathea, an honorable counsellor, a disciple of Jesus, " but secretly, for fear of the Jews." He was convinced that

Jesus was the Messiah, and designed, when he should be acknowledged and proclaimed as such, to profess his faith in him; but God gave him grace to declare his faith sooner than he designed. This honorable man was a sincere but a timid and faint-hearted disciple, and it is indeed wonderful to see how heroic he became in professing his attachment to a dead Christ, whom living he had not had courage to own. But it is substantially so now. Some men indulge the hope that they are Christians, or that God has been gracious to their souls, and yet delay to make an open profession of their faith. They in effect conceal their love for God and their hope of salvation through fear of their fellow men. This is a dangerous practice. It is contrary to the plainest commands of God our Saviour. He has again and again told us, we must take up the cross and follow him. If we are ashamed of him before men, he will be ashamed of us before his Father and his holy angels. If we do really love him, we will keep his commandments. If we have satisfactory evidence that Jesus is Christ, we have no right to withhold our testimony in his behalf. We have no right to hide our light under a bushel; nor is it to be expected that we shall have any comfort in religion, if we do not obey all the known commandments of God. What, then, are the commandments of God which are unto life? We must at least have faith in him and in his word, and to discern the Lord's body, before we are prepared to take the holy sacrament. Christ says: "Do this in remembrance of me." But you say: How can I know whether or not I am prepared to obey this command? We answer by asking you, Do you believe in your heart that Jesus Christ is the Son of God and the Saviour of sinners, as he is set forth in the Gospel? Do you feel that you are a sinner in the sight of God, and that you must trust in Christ or perish in your sins? And are you resolved, by the help of God, that you will forsake all known sins and try to live a Christian life? As far as you know yourself, do you accept of Jesus Christ as the only Saviour, and put all your trust in him? Then we say, Come and welcome. Come to the Lord's supper, and whosoever cometh unto Him shall be saved.

IX.

PAUL'S VOYAGE AND SHIPWRECK.

And when it was determined that we should sail into Italy, they delivered Paul, and certain other prisoners, unto *one* named Julius, a centurion of Augustus' band. And, entering into a ship of Adramyttium, we launched, meaning to sail by the coast of Asia; one Aristarchus, a Macedonian of Thessalonica, being with us. And the next day we touched at Sidon. And Julius courteously entreated Paul, and gave him liberty to go unto his friends to refresh himself. And when we had launched from thence, we sailed under Cyprus, because the winds were contrary. And when we had sailed over the sea of Cilicia and Pamphilia, we came to Myra, a city of Lycia. And there the centurion found a ship of Alexandria sailing into Italy; and he put us therein. And when we had sailed slowly many days, and scarce were come over against Cnidus, the wind not suffering us, we sailed under Crete, over against Salmone; and, hardly passing it, came unto a place which is called The Fair Havens; nigh whereunto was the city of Lasea.

Now when much time was spent, and when sailing was now dangerous, because the fast was now already past, Paul admonished them, and said unto them, Sirs, I perceive that this voyage will be with hurt and much damage, not only of the lading and ship, but also of our lives. Nevertheless the centurion believed the master and the owner of the ship, more than those things which were spoken by Paul. And because the haven was not commodious to winter in, the more part advised to depart thence also, if by any means they might attain to Phenice, and there to winter; which is a haven of Crete, and lieth toward the southwest and northwest. And when the south wind blew softly, supposing that they had obtained their purpose, loosing thence, they sailed close by Crete. But not long after there arose against it a tempestuous wind, called Euroclydon.

And when the ship was caught, and could not bear up into the wind, we let her drive. And running under a certain island which is called Clauda, we had much work to come by the boat: which when they had taken up, they used helps, undergirding the ship; and, fearing lest they should fall into the quicksands, strake sail, and so were driven. And we being exceedingly tossed with a tempest, the next day they lightened the ship; and the third day we cast out with our own hands the tackling of the ship. And when neither sun nor stars in many days appeared, and no small tempest lay on us, all hope that we should be saved was then taken away.

But after long abstinence, Paul stood forth in the midst of them, and said, Sirs, ye should have hearkened unto me, and not have loosed from Crete, and to have gained this harm and loss. And now I exhort you to be of good cheer: for there shall be no loss of any man's life among you, but of the ship. For there stood by me this night the angel of God, whose I am, and whom I serve, saying, Fear not, Paul:

thou must be brought before Cesar: and, lo, God hath given thee all them that sail with thee. Wherefore, sirs, be of good cheer: for I believe God, that it shall be even as it was told me. Howbeit we must be cast upon a certain island. But when the fourteenth night was come, as we were driven up and down in Adria, about midnight the shipmen deemed that they drew near to some country; and sounded, and found it twenty fathoms: and when they had gone a little further, they sounded again, and found it fifteen fathoms. Then fearing lest they should have fallen upon rocks, they cast four anchors out of the stern, and wished for the day. And as the shipmen were about to flee out of the ship, when they had let down the boat into the sea, under color as though they would have cast anchors out of the foreship, Paul said to the centurion and the soldiers, Except these abide in the ship, ye cannot be saved. Then the soldiers cut off the ropes of the boat, and let her fall off. And while the day was coming on, Paul besought them all to take meat, saying, This day is the fourteenth day that ye have tarried and continued fasting, having taken nothing. Wherefore I pray you to take some meat: for this is for your health: for there shall not a hair fall from the head of any of you. And when he had thus spoken, he took bread, and gave thanks to God in presence of them all: and when he had broken it, he began to eat. Then were they all of good cheer, and they also took some meat. And we were in all in the ship two hundred threescore and sixteen souls. And when they had eaten enough, they lightened the ship, and cast out the wheat into the sea. And when it was day, they knew not the land: but they discovered a certain creek with a shore, into the which they were minded, if it were possible, to thrust in the ship. And when they had taken up the anchors, they committed *themselves* unto the sea, and loosed the rudder bands, and hoisted up the mainsail to the wind, and made toward shore. And falling into a place where two seas met, they ran the ship aground; and the forepart stuck fast, and remained unmovable, but the hinder part was broken with the violence of the waves. And the soldiers' counsel was to kill the prisoners, lest any of them should swim out, and escape. But the centurion, willing to save Paul, kept them from their purpose; and commanded that they which could swim should cast themselves first into the sea, and get to land: and the rest, some on boards, and some on broken pieces of the ship. And so it came to pass, that they escaped all safe to land.

And when they were escaped, then they knew that the island was called Melita. And the barbarous people showed us no little kindness: for they kindled a fire, and received us every one, because of the present rain, and because of the cold. And when Paul had gathered a bundle of sticks, and laid them on the fire, there came a viper out of the heat and fastened on his hand. And when the barbarians saw the venomous beast hang on his hand, they said among themselves, No doubt this man is a murderer, whom, though he hath escaped the sea, yet vengeance suffereth not to live. And he shook off the beast into the fire, and felt no harm. Howbeit they looked when he should have swollen, or fallen down dead suddenly: but after they had looked a great while, and saw no harm come to him, they changed their minds, and said that he was a god.

In the same quarters were possessions of the chief man of the island, whose name was Publius; who received us, and lodged us three days courteously. And it came to pass, that the father of Publius lay sick of a fever and of a bloody flux: to whom Paul entered in, and prayed, and laid his hands on him, and healed him. So when this was done, others also, which had diseases in the island, came, and were healed: who also honored us with many honors; and when we departed, they laded us with such things as were necessary. And after three months we departed in a ship of Alexandria, which had wintered in the isle, whose sign was Castor and Pollux. And landing at Syracuse, we tarried there three days. And from thence we fetched a compass, and came to Rhegium: and after one day the south wind blew, and we came the next day to Puteoli: where we found brethren, and were desired to tarry with them seven days: and so we went toward Rome. And from thence, when the brethren heard of us, they came to meet us as far as Appii-forum, and The Three Taverns: whom when Paul saw, he thanked God, and took courage. And when we came to Rome, the centurion delivered the prisoners to the captain of the guard: but Paul was suffered to dwell by himself with a soldier that kept him. And it came to pass, that after three days Paul called the chief of the Jews together: and when they were come together, he said unto them, Men and brethren, though I have committed nothing against the people, or customs of our fathers, yet was I delivered prisoner from Jerusalem into the hands of the Romans. Who, when they had examined me, would have let me go, because there was no cause of death in me. But when the Jews spake against it, I was constrained to appeal unto Cæsar; not that I had aught to accuse my nation of. For this cause therefore have I called for you, to see you, and to speak with you: because that for the hope of Israel I am bound with this chain. And they said unto him, We neither received letters out of Judea concerning thee, neither any of the brethren that came showed or spake any harm of thee. But we desire to hear of thee what thou thinkest: for as concerning this sect, we know that everywhere it is spoken against. And when they had appointed him a day, there came many to him into his lodging; to whom he expounded and testified the kingdom of God, persuading them concerning Jesus, both out of the law of Moses, and out of the prophets, from morning till evening. And some believed the things which were spoken, and some believed not. And when they agreed not among themselves, they departed, after that Paul had spoken one word, Well spake the Holy Ghost by Esaias the prophet unto our fathers, saying, Go unto this people, and say, Hearing ye shall hear, and shall not understand; and seeing ye shall see, and not perceive: for the heart of this people is waxed gross, and their ears are dull of hear ing, and their eyes have they closed; lest they should see with their eyes, and hear with their ears, and understand with their heart, and should be converted, and I should heal them. Be it known therefore unto you, that the salvation of God is sent unto the Gentiles, and that they will hear it. And when he had said these words, the Jews departed, and had great reasoning among themselves. And Paul dwelt two whole years in his own hired house, and received all that came in unto him, preaching the kingdom of God, and teaching those things which concern the Lord Jesus Christ, with all confidence, no man forbidding him. *Acts* xxvii. *and* xxviii.

X.

JULIUS, THE CENTURION OF PAUL'S VOYAGE TO ROME.

The island of Paul's shipwreck was called Melita, which we have no doubt is the Malta of our times. Almost all the local traditions of Malta, about Paul and the incidents or circumstances of the voyage, and of the wrecking of the vessel as given in the Acts, are approved of by Dr. Kitto, Mr. Smith, of Jordan-Hill, and by other recent and able writers.* So well

---

* A knowledge of the ships and navigation of the ancients, and of the form and structure of Greek and Roman vessels, and of the way in which they were worked, and of the trade and travel carried on in the apostle's day between Alexandria and Europe, removes many of the difficulties that at first seem to rise up in the minds of inquiring students as they read the history of Paul's voyage to Rome. In the great and scholarly works of the late Admiral Sir Charles Penrose, and also of James Smith, Esq., and of Conybeare and Howson, this whole subject has been ably treated. The eye of a sailor and the pen of the scholar have been so united in these works for the elucidation of the voyage and wrecking of the apostle, that but little more can be desired.

satisfied are we of this, that we consider it time lost to refute the opinion that the island of the shipwreck was Venice or Meleda in Dalmatia. The Malta of our day was the Melita of the Acts. Nor is there any difficulty about *Adria*, for the Adriatic sea, according to ancient usage, means all the Mediterranean between Greece on the one side and Italy and Sicily on the other. It was sometimes called the Gulf of Adria.

And when it was determined—decided upon by Festus the Roman governor. This does not mean, however, that any violence was done either to the free-agency of the apostle or of the Roman governor. It was God's purpose that Paul should stand before Cæsar in Rome; and for the fulfilling of that purpose, the apostle himself is left free to make his appeal to the emperor, and the authorities acting according to their own judgment and pleasure determined to send him. *We* probably means Paul, Timothy, Aristarchus, and Luke the writer, as well as other prisoners. Paul's companions were not sent as criminals or prisoners, but went as his friends and fellow laborers who felt a deep sympathy for him, and thus desired to show their love for the cause in which he was laboring and for which he suffered so much. This Aristarchus is probably the same who is mentioned *Col.* iv. 10, and if so, for some cause or other, he was also made at a subsequent time the apostle's fellow-prisoner. The centurion of Capernaum, and the centurion in command at the crucifixion, saw and heard the Lord Jesus themselves in the days of his flesh; but Cornelius, the centurion of Cesarea, and Julius, the centurion who had charge of Paul during his voyage and shipwreck on his way to Rome, do not appear to have known anything of our Lord except what they learned from the apostles Peter and Paul. And though this fact may seem scarcely worthy of note, it is not without signification. For it proves to us that the Gospel preached by Christ's ministers has the same effect that it had when preached by himself. And this is according to his promise and to his prayer in behalf of all who should hear of him and believe upon him through the Word; that is, the doctrines which he commanded his ministering servants to teach and preach in all the world. Accordingly, when Peter preached to the centurion at Cesarea, and Paul became acquainted with the centurion who had charge of him to take him to Rome, we suppose the effect was similar to that produced on those who saw our Lord's miracles and witnessed his conduct amid his sufferings and in death.

1. The circumstances under which we first make the acquaintance of the centurion Julius, the Roman officer in command during the voyage and shipwreck of Paul on his way to Rome, are worthy of consideration. When the ship struck and was about to be dashed to pieces by the violence of the sea, we find the military authority of Rome on board the wrecking ship. A number of prisoners were crowded together in that ship on their way to the imperial city. It was natural at such a time that every one should try to save himself, and that the prisoners should not only save themselves from a grave in the sea, but escape also from their

keepers. But the soldiers knowing that if this should happen they would be blamed, proposed to put the prisoners to death to prevent the possibility of censure for their escape. Here it is that the centurion Julius arrests our attention. Being in command, his authority is used to prevent the killing of the prisoners. Not that he was less familiar than his soldiers to deeds of cruelty and blood, but because of his regard for Paul. He does not seem to have had any care for the lives of the other prisoners, but wishing to save Paul, he kept them from their purpose.—*Acts* xxvii. 43.

But why did the centurion desire to save the apostle? We are told when it was decided that Paul should be sent into Italy, that he was delivered with other prisoners " unto one named Julius, a centurion of Augustus' band, and that when the ship touched at Sidon," Julius courteously entreated Paul, and gave him liberty to go unto his friends to refresh himself. *Verses* 1–3. Here is a happy contrast. A military officer shows more kindness to the apostle than his own countrymen, or the civil authorities have done. Felix and Festus and the Jews were unreasonable in their enmity and prejudices. But should we not expect, in the military profession, and on the part of those who are educated to be gentlemen and to have the command of bodies of men, and to be intrusted with the most important events and negotiations, such lofty sentiments, such a keen sense of honor, and such nobleness and generosity as to overcome all prejudice, and to treat those in their power not only with justice but with kindness. This we are prepared to expect from this man's education and profession, and such was in fact the conduct of all the centurions referred to in the Gospel.

Julius belonged to Augustus' band—Cohors Augusta—was the emperor's body guard. *Lepsius on Tacitus*, His. lib. ii., says he has identified the very name of this cohort on an ancient marble. (See also Suetonius' Nero.) This band, therefore, has no reference to the city of Sebaste, but to service in immediate connection with the emperor. It was a cohort belonging particularly to the emperor, or had charge of his palace and person. Julius, then, was not an ordinary officer. He had been selected because of his eminent character and services for a post of peculiar trust. He must then have possessed more intelligence than most others; was no doubt well acquainted with the world; a good judge of men; has travelled and read much; conversed with the most intelligent of many countries and nations; is qualified to give information and advice at a moment's notice to the emperor. He has been to Judea, and is now returning to Rome, and the prisoners are put under his care. He was able at once to see that Paul, though a man of rather small stature and no great bodily presence, was, however, no common man. Paul was now full of years. Has been a minister of Jesus Christ for nearly thirty years. And as a man's appearance, his expression of face, is modified by the society he keeps, the business he follows, and more than all by the sentiments he indulges, so no doubt to some extent the apostle's countenance was an index to his principles and feelings. There are of course exceptions, but somehow or other religious creeds are seen even in the shape and expression of men's faces. Long continued thought and deep feelings mould the countenance. Paul's face, then, must by this time have beamed with lofty motives and heavenly hopes. Nor would such an observing officer as this centurion fail to become acquainted with the malice of his enemies, or to have heard of the selfishness and bribery of his judges, nor would he overlook the zeal and self-denial, and ungrudging, whole-hearted devotion of the apostle to the service of Christ. How long the centurion has been absent from Rome we do not know; nor how long he was at Cesarea; but it is probable as Paul was a Roman citizen, and had been two years in prison at Cesarea, that he had learned something of him before the voyage commenced. And as Paul was famed for learning and eloquence, and had several times been permitted to make an oration in his behalf, it is not at all impossible—but is indeed very probable—that Julius had at some time heard the apostle plead his cause before some of the distinguished persons of Cesarea;

had heard the wonderful story of his conversion; and how he had been persecuted, and was still willing to preach and suffer and die for the faith he had once endeavored to destroy. It is not asking too much to believe that he was more or less acquainted with Paul's history before he received him as a prisoner to be conveyed to Rome. And as a man of the world, with the clear eye of a well-educated and travelled officer, and comparatively without the malice or prejudices of sects or race, he was satisfied that Paul was a man greatly misrepresented and abused, and was a man of an extraordinary character. He could see that Paul was a man of great learning and of intellectual power; that he was not ignorant, vain, self-conceited, nor morbid, nor devoted to pleasure, nor the seeking of fame nor power. He felt satisfied that his motives were pure; that he was neither knave nor fanatic. There was something about the apostle that at once attracted the intelligent Roman officer's kind regards, and this impression would only be the deeper, if he had previously learned anything of his character or of his doctrines that caused him to feel a peculiar interest in him, and wish to preserve his life for their sake. What was it, then, that attracted the kind regards of the Roman officer? It could not have been his sacerdotal character. For Paul was not of the Levitical tribe, nor did he wear priestly robes. Indeed it would seem that but few Jewish priests, but few of the tribe of Levi, ever became Gospel ministers. We read in *Acts* vi. 7, that a great company of the priests were obedient to the faith; but we do not hear of them again. There is no record of any of them having become Christian ministers. At all events Paul was not a priest. There is in fact but one priest who has power to mediate between God and man: the "great High Priest, who has passed into the heavens." The Church has had prophets and apostles, and now has evangelists, pastors and teachers, but only one priest— Jesus Christ. It was not, therefore, because Paul claimed any peculiar attention as a priest that the centurion desired to save him.

The Adramittium of the narrative was not

Hadrumatum of Africa, as some say, and have thereby brought confusion into the history, but the Adramittium of Asia Minor. At Myra of Lycia, a flourishing seaport in Asia Minor, the centurion transfers the prisoners into a ship laden with corn, bound from Alexandria to Rome. This was a large ship—five hundred tons—having on board, beside her cargo, two hundred and seventy-six persons. The voyage with corn from Egypt, which was then the granary of the Roman Empire, to Italy was a common one, and this course from Alexandria to Puteoli the ordinary one. Lardner has also proved that it was common at this time to send prisoners from Judea and other provinces to Rome. Nor was it strange that this vessel was found at Lycia, for not having the compass, they pursued a circuitous route, scarcely ever going out of sight of land.

The progress of this vessel seems to have been beset with many dangers. And by and by, we find the centurion following the advice of the master and owner rather than taking the counsel of Paul. This was natural. Paul was neither owner nor pilot, nor was he an old mariner. The centurion may have thought this is a subject out of his line; but still he found, in the end, that Paul was right, even about navigating the ship.

Read here *verses* 9, 10, 11, 12 of chapter xxvii.

As nearly as we can make it out, the case was on this wise: The direct course of the ship would have been along the north coast of the island of Candia, anciently called Crete. This island is about forty miles broad and one hundred and eighty miles long. It would, therefore, have been a guide to the mariners for at least two hundred miles. But the wind blowing from the northwest, instead of going along the northern shore of this island, they steered under its shelter on the south side, until they passed Salmone and came to a place called Fair Havens. Here a difference of opinion arises as to what should be done. As they had neither compass nor steam, and the winter was upon them, and the safe season for navigating the Mediterranean was over, it was proposed to spend the winter there or at some port on the southern coast of Candia, or to double Cape Matala, and try to get to Phenice, some fifty miles farther, where there was a more commodious harbor. Paul advised them to remain at Fair Havens; but the opinion of the master and ship-owner prevailed, and they attempted to reach Phenice, and with what result we shall soon see. Accordingly they hoist anchor and give their sails to the breeze for the port of Phenice, and with a few hours of fair wind would have reached it; but a typhoon comes after them from the northeast, and it is in vain they try to get to the desired haven. All they can do is to let the vessel scud—drive before the wind—and instead of gaining Phenice, they come up under the lee of Clauda, an island twenty or thirty miles south of Phenice. But now something must be done, for they are rushing to certain destruction on the quicksands of Africa. But it seems that then as now, every ship had a boat or boats, and that as the ships in those times for the most part crept along the coast and kept up an almost every day's communication with the land, so the boat was not taken up and secured on deck as with us at the commencement of the voyage, but was kept on the water attached to the stern by a rope, ready for use, as we have often seen them tied to the steamers on the Mississippi River. Hence we are told that they secured the boat—that is, took it upon board the vessel so as to keep it from being swamped, and "undergirded the ship"*—"frapped it," which means passing strong ropes under and around her hull, to strengthen and prevent her from springing a leak or going to pieces under the blows of the heavy seas that struck her.

Then they "strake sail,"† that is, set the

---

* Lord Anson, in his voyage round the world, speaking of a Spanish man of war in a storm, says, "they were obliged to throw overboard all their upper-deck guns, and take six turns of the cable round the ship, to prevent her opening." Other cases are also cited in the books.

† Several expressions are used here that are obscure. It is evident they lightened the ship by casting over the cumbrous wares. The *tackling* means anchors, cables and baggage not absolutely necessary. By *straking sail* is probably meant letting down the mast, or cutting it away. They were already under bare poles.

storm sails so as to steady the vessel, and steered as nearly as they could in a northwesterly course. But on the third day, the tempest continuing violent, they threw overboard the heavy tackling of the ship. This proves that she was now leaking, and that they judged it necessary to lighten her as much as possible. Then followed many days of darkness and most painful uncertainty. Neither sun nor stars appeared—no compass—no vision of land. They knew not what moment they might be dashed to pieces on rocks, or driven on a lee shore. The vessel is strained more and more, and the leaking increases. If she is not dashed to pieces, she must soon sink in the waves. What wild emotions—what feelings, fears or hopes must have filled the minds of this crowd of two hundred and seventy-six persons, as they contemplated the prospect of being wrecked on some unknown coast! But now we see the blessing of having a man of God on board. One whose heart is stayed upon God, and can hold intercourse with heaven by prayer.

PAUL'S VISION.

2. "But after long abstinence, Paul stood forth in the midst of them, and said, Sirs, ye should have hearkened unto me, and not have loosed from Crete, and to have gained this harm and loss. And now I exhort you to be of good cheer: for there shall be no loss of any man's life among you, but of the ship. For there stood by me this night the angel of God, whose I am and whom I serve, saying, Fear not, Paul; thou must be brought before Cæsar; and lo, God hath given thee all them that sail with thee. Wherefore, sirs, be of good cheer: for I believe God, that it shall be even as it was told me. Howbeit, we must be cast upon a certain island."

Whose I am, with the correlative, *whom I serve*, is the whole of religion. To belong to God is the height of our faith and happiness. Every blessing is comprehended in this—that we are God's, and that we serve him with all our mind and with all our soul and with all our strength. Surely these were glad tidings—good news, and emphatic, too, every one is to be saved—not one of the two hundred and seventy-six persons on board is to be lost by the wreck. They were all sinners, and all except three or four, heathens, yet all are to be saved for the sake of Paul, the servant of Jesus Christ. The wicked are often delivered from temporal afflictions for the sake of the pious among whom they live. The tares are allowed to grow for the sake of the wheat. This was God's gracious opportunity. It was man's extremity. Helpless, comfortless, cheerless, hopeless—it was God's favored moment to appear for the help of his servants. "And God shall help her, and that right early," that is most opportunely. And we have here also an illustration of the apostle's sincerity and boldness. For if he is not truly authorized as a messenger of heaven to make such a promise—if he is deceived himself, or is seeking to impose upon others—soon his prophecy will fail and destroy his reputation and show that the faith he professed is a miserable delusion. But he says, I know that it shall be just as I have said, for "there stood by me this night the angel of God," and I know it shall be as God has said. Two things here must have arrested the attention of the other prisoners, and especially the master and ship-owner; namely, that they had made a mistake about leaving Fair Havens, and that Paul's sagacity as a seaman was to be relied on more than theirs; and, secondly, that now he had what they had not, a communication from the Supreme Being—"the angel of God, whom he served"—had declared to him the particulars of their escape which he had gladly announced to them. For the apostle was careful to let them know that it was not from his own natural sagacity or superior seamanship, nor by magic or witchcraft, that he was able to give them so joyful an assurance, but that it was from the God of heaven whom he served. He honors his blessed master by telling them that all he knew on the subject had been revealed to him. The centurion must now have felt more than ever an interest in him, when he discovered that he held direct communication with heaven. If he was favorably impressed

with his prisoner when he first received him at
Cesarea—if he felt an interest in him because
of his learning, eloquence, sincerity and zeal,
or because he seemed to him to be a persecuted
man, having a clear head, an honest heart and
a good conscience, how much more may we
suppose that he felt concerned for his safety,
when he saw that he was filled with the inspiration of the most high God? If he had
admired him before, because his skill and knowledge had enabled him to give an advice about
wintering at Fair Havens, which was better
than the opinion of the owner of the ship, and
wiser than all the wisdom of the army and
navy on board the ship, how much more must
he have reverenced him now as one whose wisdom was directly from heaven? And must he
not also have been constrained to believe that
the religion taught by such a man was the true
religion?

And the history is the more remarkable just
here, because it shows how completely Paul,
though a prisoner, is now the actual master of
the vessel. In fact, he is in command, and not

the ship's master nor the captain of the guard. It was under Paul's orders the soldiers cut the ropes of the boat and let her fall into the sea, thereby seeming to deprive themselves of the best, if not the only means left for effecting their escape. Here, again, we see how *true courage makes one a majority.* We see how completely a man of mind—one mind self-possessed and stout-hearted, and at perfect peace with itself, and stayed upon God, gains an ascendency over others. Truly, it was sublime. Paul the despised Jew—the prisoner under various charges in custody of soldiers—on his way to the Mamertine dungeons—yes, this is the man who, when all on board are exhausted by anxiety, fear, toil and fasting, stands up and says: "I pray you," excellent sirs, master, shipowner, Roman commandant, and soldiers and mariners, fellow prisoners—all of you, "I pray you take some meat: for this is for your health: for there shall not a hair fall from the head of any of you." "Then were they all of good cheer, and they also took some meat." This was probably the only thing like a meal they had taken since the beginning of the storm. And after thus refreshing themselves, we find them again using the means that seemed best calculated to secure their escape. They lightened the ship by casting the corn into the sea. Nor could it at this time have escaped so intelligent a man as the centurion, to observe how much more confident and composed the apostle was than the rest of the company. He alone could say anything hopeful. He alone could say: "Sirs, be of good cheer: for I believe God, that it shall be even as it was told me." Blessed indeed is the gift of faith. Blessed is he that believes God! This is happiness. This is a refuge that never fails. Here is the source of true courage. The heart stayed upon God can well afford to be magnanimous cheerful, fearless. "I fear God, and know *no other* fear," is truly sublime.*

1. *The accuracy of Paul's prediction is remarkable.* The vessel was to be lost, and they were to be cast upon a certain island, yet not a soul on board was to perish. He himself was

---

* " Je crains Dieu, et n'ai point d'autre crainte."

to be brought before the emperor. It might have seemed probable that they would be wrecked on an island where there were so many, and that a few of the persons would be saved, but who could confidently declare that every one on the ship should escape from a watery grave? This prediction he could not have made without divine authority. But each and every particular of the prophecy was verified.

2. The conversion of Paul has long been regarded by Lord Littleton and others as one of the strongest arguments in behalf of Christianity. But if the argument from his conversion is so irresistible now, why was it not equally so when the centurion was made acquainted with it from the apostle's own lips? Surely, the demonstration of the truth of the religion he professed from his own account of his conversion when it was accompanied by prophecies and miracles that proved him to be in communication with God, could not have been weaker than it is now. We should think the conviction on such a mind as that of the centurion, under all the circumstances,

must been very strongly in favor of Christianity.

3. Let us observe also in this history a remarkable illustration of the philosophical Bible truth, *that God is sovereign and man is free.* The apostle pointedly declares to the centurion: " Except these abide in the ship, ye cannot be saved." *Verse* 31. By which we understand the apostle at one blow to cut the Gordian knot about sovereignty and free agency. He has declared that the angel of God has told him that every soul is to be saved from the violence of the sea, and he " believes God that it shall be even as it was told him ;" yet here he says, the means adapted to prevent our perishing must be used: " These must abide in the ship, or ye cannot be saved." The end and the means must always go together. They are always so in the divine mind. To trust to means is to despise God, and to neglect the use of the means he has appointed is presumptuous; is wicked; is to tempt God. It was God's purpose that all should be saved from death at that time, and in order to this result

it was his purpose they should all remain in the ship. "Almighty God," says the pious Burkitt, "likes not to be tied to means himself, but it is his pleasure to tie us. Sometimes, to show his sovereignty, he is pleased to work without means; sometimes, to show his omnipotence, he works against means. The fire shall not burn, the water shall not drown, the iron shall swim, the sun shall stand still. THE FIRST CAUSE can suspend the power of second causes when he pleases. But as the care of the end belongs to God, so the care of the means belongs to us, and must be used when they may, and where they can be used. Accordingly here the mariners, in order to their own and others' preservation, stay in the ship, lighten it, undergird it, cast out their anchors, hoist up the mainsail, loose the rudder-bands, and do everything to their preservation which was needful. The purpose of God to prolong our lives must not lessen our care for the preservation of our lives: when God has ordained and appointed means, we cannot expect to find safety in the neglect of those means." Human means are not to be neglected because we have gracious and sovereign promises, but the rather to be diligently used. The certainty of an event as seen by God does not render it improper for us to use the means. The determining of the event comprehends the means requisite to effect it. And it is our duty to use these means as they are put into our power and according to the divine directions, just as diligently as if we could save ourselves, and then to trust in the grace of God as wholly as if we could do nothing at all. Salvation is of free grace, through the appointed means.

4. We have here an illustration of the *benefits of being in good company.* For Paul's sake the rest of the prisoners were saved from death, either from a watery grave or from a summary execution by the soldiers. One sinner destroyeth much good. The companion of fools shall be destroyed. But ten righteous men would have saved Sodom. For the elect's sake the evil days are shortened. Let young people then remember that human history is full of illustrations of the truth of the fable that

teaches the danger of bad company. The lessons of our streets and of every-day life demonstrate its truth. Common sense as well as the Bible warns us to beware of evil doers.

5. If you ask us whether or not Julius, the centurion of Paul's voyage and shipwreck, became a Christian, we answer that our history is altogether silent on the subject. We cannot answer categorically; but we hope he did. It is seen from our examination of the narration, that he was under the influence of a man full of faith and of the Holy Ghost; of an apostle who was intent, like his great master, not to destroy men's lives, but to save them; and to save them not only from death temporal, but from everlasting death. And we have seen that there are circumstances in the centurion's connection with the apostle well calculated to convince him that the apostle's religion was different from and superior to that of the Jews and Romans; that by having direct intercourse with heaven, he was clothed with credentials that asserted the truth of the religion he professed; and we have found that as a centurion

of the royal Augustan cohort, he must have been a favorite officer, a man of superior merit, probably on account of his learning, experience and talents; that he was intelligent and well travelled, and possessed of a mind comparatively free from prejudice and well disciplined. What then is to hinder our belief that he was converted to Christianity? He certainly had every opportunity to know the truth. Not only had he been in the Holy Land, and been made somewhat acquainted with the facts of our Lord's life, death, and resurrection, and of Paul's conversion; for we cannot suppose such a man to have travelled from Rome to Judea at that time, without having learned more or less about these things; and then he is in daily contact with Paul on the voyage, and has an opportunity of hearing him preach for some three months that they remained on the island, where probably every day Paul was the chaplain of the cohort and of his fellow-prisoners and of the crew. The centurion must have known of Paul's miracle, and of his influence among the people of Melita. Nor can we believe that Paul failed to take pains, as far as was becoming in a prisoner, to acquaint him with the character of Christ and the proofs of his Messiahship. And then we must remember that the last mention we have in the sacred narrative of the centurion, like the first, is connected with kindness toward the apostle. When they all reached Rome, *chap.* xxviii. 16, the centurion delivered his prisoners to the captain of the guard, and Paul was allowed to dwell by himself with a soldier that kept him. This is recorded as a special favor granted to the apostle, and was doubtless secured for him by the influence of the centurion. And so we have no doubt the unusual liberty and kindness shown to Paul, when he was allowed to dwell two years in his own hired house in Rome, and received all that came to him, preaching the kingdom of God, and teaching those things which concern the Lord Jesus Christ, with all confidence, no man forbidding him; that all this was obtained for him by the centurion's favorable report of his character and conduct. It is not then, we trust, presuming on history, to hope that, like the jailer of Philippi, he inquired what he should do to be saved, and receiving a similar answer, was made a partaker of the great salvation.

6. Deliverances from the perils of a journey by land or of a sea voyage, and especially from the dangers of a battle or of a shipwreck, call for special thanksgiving, and increased devotion to God and the things of eternity.

7. We should not allow ourselves to be discouraged because we meet with difficulties in the way of duty. Joseph was a favorite with his father and with heaven, yet his early years were crowded with what the world calls bad luck or sad mishaps. Esther is left an orphan in captivity, but her God prepares her for the crown of Persia, and then places it on her head, and brings her to the kingdom to deliver his church and save his people from their enemies. The Hebrews are in the way of duty, though just after they leave Egypt they are shut in at the Red Sea. Difficulties at the beginning of a journey or of a voyage, or at the opening of a new business, are no

signs that it is not going to turn out prosperously. The proverb is, that "a bad beginning has a good end;" and in the sense of meeting with hindrances or obstacles, it may be regarded as true. The omens of Paul's voyage were both good and bad. The worst feature about it was the bad company with whom he was to make a long voyage. Many a convict from Great Britain to Botany Bay was comparatively innocent at the beginning of the voyage to what he was when he arrived at its end. The associations of the voyage were from bad to worse all the way. And so the corruption, the utter loss of shame and of self-respect, has often been completed, and the way to ruin hastened by confining juvenile offenders with those that were more skilled and hardened in crime. To a man of the education and refinement of Paul, a long voyage with such prisoners and soldiers must have been a severe trial. But it was a kind Providence that put such a gentleman as the Roman officer, Julius, in command of the guard on that ship. Paul had appealed to Rome and was to stand before Cæsar, thinking that, as he was a Roman citizen, he could find justice there rather than among his own countrymen, or at the court of the pro-consul at Cesarea; but his voyage was in many respects one of the most disagreeable and dangerous on record. Nevertheless it was God's will that he should testify of Jesus at Rome. It was not then because Paul was on board that there was a storm and the vessel was lost. Paul was in the way of duty, yet everything seemed to be working against him. The Jews laid in wait for him, and when he had escaped their hands, then contrary winds and waves are against him. The malice of his enemies, the unreasonable prejudice of his own countrymen, and the wars of the elements, are all permitted to work against him; yet they were all overruled. They all worked together for his good. And if no adverse circumstances had followed this voyage, if no Divine interferences, no shipwreck and no miracles, then there had been no church at Malta. "The Lord hath indeed prepared his throne in the heavens, and his kingdom ruleth over all." "He maketh the wrath of man to praise him, and the remainder he restraineth." God can make all occurrences and events promote the welfare of his holy Church. Why then should we not leave the government of the world in his hands, and trust most lovingly to his gracious promises? Hitherto he hath done all things well. And his wisdom, power, and goodness are as ample for the future as they were for the past. The absolute assurance, however, of God's promises is never to be construed into a neglect of the appointed means. It is God's plan to work by miracles when ordinary means are used to the utmost. "The gods help those who help themselves." The Divine promise is, that God's presence shall always go with his servants. The Lord God is a sun and a shield; he will give grace and glory, and no good thing will he withhold from them that walk uprightly. He can raise up friends for them in the darkest hours, and from the most unexpected sources. When he allows them to be sent to prison, he will send his angel with them, and give them a keeper such as he sees it is best for them to have, and give them favor in the sight of their keepers. And if, as in this case, saints and sinners are mixed together, crowded up on board the same ship, still God knows his people and will make a great difference between them and those that serve him not. The special, gracious presence of God is a sufficient and sure support for his people under all the trials of life. It was no doubt a great comfort to the apostle, that he had such companions as Timothy and Aristarchus for the whole, or even a part of this voyage, and that he was permitted to land at Sidon and see the brethren there, and receive refreshments and supplies from them for his tedious voyage; and that at Puteoli, having escaped the perils of the wreck, he should find brethren who entertained him seven days, and thence on his voyage to Rome, till he met other brethren who came to meet him "as far as Appii Forum and the Three Taverns, whom when Paul saw, he thanked God, and took courage." And after his arrival in the imperial city, his greatest joy was to write to the churches and to preach Jesus and the resurrection, and salvation through him, both to Jews and Gentiles. But how blessed, how much more triumphant his departure to the New Jerusalem, which is above, the eternal city of God! Then he finished his course with joy, and put on his crown of glory and immortality.

"Dear Jesus grant when our work is done,
When the battle's fought, the race is run,
We may hear thy voice calling us home,
　　　　Across the River.

"And though its waves may be dark and cold,
May our hope be bright, our faith be bold,
'Till we are gathered safely in thy fold
　　　　Across the River."
—*Mrs. C. D. S. in the* "*Pacific Expositor.*"

XI.

THE CHOICE OF A CALLING OR PROFESSION.*

Lord, what wilt thou have me to do?—*Acts* ix. 6.

THE three grand essentials to our chief end, which is happiness in this life and in the world to come, or as the catechism more definitely and forcibly expresses it, "to glorify God and enjoy him forever," are something to do, something to love, and something to hope for. And in finding this something to do, to love and to hope for, and in this doing, loving and hoping, is the battle of life. And a great battle it is. To be born into life is a victory, and to die is a battle, but whether unto victory or defeat depends upon the manner of our life. All the

---

* This is taken from a discourse entitled: "Some thoughts on the principles which should guide a young man in the choice of a calling or profession, delivered in Calvary Church, San Francisco, Sabbath evening, 14th April, 1861, as the fifth of the series before the Young Men's Christian Association. By Rev. Dr. Scott."

way, however, from the cradle and our first campaign into the world, to the coffin and our last campaign, when we leave the field, it is all a battle. Nor can it be otherwise. Nor is it desirable it should be otherwise. Nor is it wise or manly to deplore that it is so.

Life is a battle, a stern battle, that must be fought, and fought all the way up hill and against an enemy's batteries. But were it not so, where were the glory of success? If there was nothing to struggle against, where were the honor of winning? Opposition stimulates courage; difficulties enhance the glory of success, until, as the poet says, "Danger's self is lure alone." It is only the coward who sinks into the dust because a lion is found in the path, or a mountain avalanche has fallen across the road. A close view, if his eye is fixed only on going ahead in the right way, will show him that the lion is chained, or that there is a way over the mountain. There is no lion in the way of duty that does not quail before an honest eye and a bold heart. It is not only true, as General Jackson said, that "true courage makes one a majority," but it is true the brave "never surrender." They never die. The flames may turn their goods to ashes or consume their dwellings. The waves may swallow up their ships. Thieves may rob their safes and carry off their gold; but the truly brave are never conquered. When they fall it is to live again. Their principles live. Their example is imperishable. The Sage of Marshfield, in his own dying words, *still lives*. Even on earth they generally win more than they lose. The highest and purest happiness is found in a firm adherence to principle and a faithful discharge of duty. Having ascertained our duty, then, we must perform it. It is more than life. We must conscientiously and scrupulously live up to our principles, if we would be happy. The consequences of doing our duty belong to God. An analysis of the text gives us three points that may help us to open up our theme, which is SOME THOUGHTS ON THE PRINCIPLES WHICH SHOULD GUIDE A YOUNG MAN IN CHOOSING AN EMPLOYMENT OR CALLING FOR LIFE.

First. The text shows that God's power is absolute over all creatures and agencies, and that it is sometimes displayed with the design of saving, when, to our view, it would seem that his purpose was to destroy. Saul was struck down, not to die, but to be raised up again a new man, that he might become Paul the apostle of the Gentiles.

Second. We have here the sincere prayer and earnest cry of a truly converted man, *Lord, what wilt thou have me to do?*

It is not what shall my neighbor do; but what wilt thou have *me* to do? It is not what wilt thou have me to *say*, but what wilt thou have me *to do?* It is not the man of professions merely, the talker and maker of fair promises that is the Christian; but he that doeth the will of God. The true inquiry of every renewed heart is to know the mind and will of God, and then to conform to it—to know his duty and do it. We may as well look to find matter without form or gravitation, or fire without heat, as to find a man converted to God without operative grace.

Third. We see that God is pleased to give an answer to the serious inquiry: "What wilt thou have me to do?" *Arise, said the Lord, and go into the city, and it shall be told thee what thou must do.* Before he was going into the city to do the devil's bloodiest work—to persecute the followers of Christ unto death. Now God tells him to go into the same city for a very different purpose. His authority, *before*, was from the high priests, and his travelling escritoire was full of commissions giving power to destroy; now his authority is from heaven, and to be instructed unto salvation for himself and for others. And although Paul's conversion and call to the ministry and apostleship are miraculous, yet his case suggests that it is a proper inquiry for every one to make: "Lord, what wilt thou have me to do?"

1. It is obvious that our choice of a pursuit, employment, calling, profession or the kind of business we are to follow by which to make a living, and in which to serve our generation, our country and our God, *should be determined by principle, and not merely from chance or the*

whims of a moment. It requires no argument to prove that young men, as free agents and rational, intelligent beings, should be governed by high correct principles in their choice of a profession for life. It is nevertheless true, that apparently trivial occurrences have exercised a controlling influence over the whole course of the lives of distinguished men. Sir Walter Scott's lameness probably had a great deal to do in shaping his habits, and enabling him to write the border tales and historic novels that have made him immortal in the English tongue. Washington's love for his mother kept him from being a sailor, and prepared him to become the leader of the American armies and the Father of his country. Joseph's many colored coat excited the envy of his brethren, who threw him into a pit till the Ishmaelites came along, and then sold him into Egypt, and the removal of Jacob and the bondage all followed. Who could have anticipated such results from Joseph's coat the bright morning he left Hebron to seek for his brethren who kept their flocks near Shechem? or who could have predicted that Moses' blow on an Egyptian's head as he was striving with a Hebrew in the field, would lead to his exile and his forty years' education in the wilderness around Mount Sinai, that was to qualify him for the great business of his life—the leading of the Hebrews out of Egypt and through that same wilderness to the borders of the promised land? But the occurrences or events that exerted a controlling influence over their whole subsequent life were small only in appearance. They were in reality great events—great because they were essential parts of "the stupendous whole" in the hands of an all-wise and Almighty Providence. They were the spring heads of a mighty stream. Although it is a part of the plan or economy of the Supreme Providence to produce great results from small beginnings, it is not true that there is any *chance* in the divine economy. All things are governed by laws. Eternal principles lie at the beginning of every man's course in life as well as in the production of the universe.

The *first* thing, then, to be known in regard

to the choice of a business for life is, that it is according to the WILL OF GOD. This is essential. For his will is the supreme law—the only infallible rule of right and wrong. No matter, therefore, how great the inducements held out to do this, or engage in that or the other business, if it involves a sin against God, or requires the violation of any of his commandments, you must not choose it. How can you sin against God, and do that great wickedness in his sight? How, then, are you to know what is according to his will? There are various methods by which we may find out what is agreeable to the will of God, but the main thing for a young man in choosing a business or profession, is to have a satisfactory answer in his own conscience to the question: "Lord, what wilt THOU have me to do?" Gifts and opportunities are to be considered, but the main question is transferred from time to eternity, from earth to heaven, and, as it were, from our own bosom to the mind of our Maker. What pursuit in life is it the will of God, who has made me, who is daily to support me, and who is to be my final Judge, that I should choose? This is the first and main question. And in seeking an answer, the first thing is to obey God in reference to our personal salvation. If any man will do the will of God, he shall know of the doctrine whether it be of God or not. What, then, is God's will? Our Lord says: He that *heareth* my word and *believeth* on him that sent me, hath everlasting life, and shall not come into condemnation; but is passed from death unto life. And when the Jews asked him, saying: What shall we do, that we might work the works of God? Jesus answered and said unto them, This is the work of God, that ye believe on him whom he hath sent. *John* v. 6. And again, we know that it is the commandment of God, that we should believe upon his only begotten Son Jesus Christ. Accordingly the disciples were sent to preach everywhere repentance toward God and faith in Christ. The first duty of every one, therefore, is to believe the testimony God has given of his Son Jesus Christ, and to accept of him as he is offered in the Gospel as our pro phet, priest and king. Until we are reconciled to God through the blood of Jesus Christ as our passover sacrificed for our sins, and feel our ignorance and need of divine illumination and guidance, we are not prepared to apprehend fully the momentous question of life: *Lord, what wilt thou have me to do?* It is then our duty first to seek the kingdom of God and his righteousness. It is *first* both in point and in importance. But how may a young man know what the will of God is? Are we to rely upon dreams, or visions, or to expect voices from heaven, or are miracles to designate the business we are to follow? By no means. The age of such miracles is past. But there are considerations which, when properly and prayerfully apprehended, will enable a young man to know what his pursuit in life should be, quite as satisfactorily as if miracles were wrought. For example, when he is debating in his mind whether he shall engage in this business, or choose this or that profession, let him ask himself: Is the business or profession which he is about to choose, the one that is the most prominent in his mind, when he is nearest to God—when he is the most humble before God and has the most exalted views of the divine character, and the profoundest reverence for the revealed will of God? Has the calling or profession he is about to choose the strongest hold upon his mind, when he fixes his eye most steadily upon death and the judgment seat? Is it the business he would prefer to be engaged in when death shall overtake him? Will it bear the light of eternity, and the scrutiny of the Judge of quick and dead? And, *secondly*, let every young man be careful that the business he selects has the approbation of his own conscience. The whole human heart is exceedingly deceitful; but the conscience is the most delicate, susceptible, sensitive organ of the human soul. It is so delicate, and so important is the moral faculty within us, that I would fain have you protect it from any abuse and from every violence. So wondrous is the moral economy under which we live, that he who cannot resist temptation is wanting in the first attribute of humanity. The very first yielding to temptation debases us. Every unrighteous deed does the actor ten thousand fold more harm than it inflicts upon the sufferer. The false man is more false to himself than to any one else. So that it is literally better to be sinned against than to sin ourselves. Better suffer ten thousand wrongs than to commit one wrong in trying to avenge ourselves. The fire of a guilty passion may scorch and wither others, but it burns the hottest at the centre, which is the sinner's own heart. And if this relation ceased at death it were not so terrible; but death only makes it worse by increasing the intensity of the woe, and adding eternity to it. Every time a man does a wrong thing, he subtracts so much from the delicacy and energy of his moral nature. And as our medical men tell us that all suffering and all violence done to our physical system, before birth, impairs our constitution, and sends us into the world shorn of much of the energy, or blunted in the fineness of the perceptions we should otherwise have possessed: so every violation of conscience in this life sends us forward into eter nity maimed and crippled, and incapable of the highest flights of bliss which we might have reached by maintaining our moral nature more perfect. "Every instance of violated conscience, like every broken string in a harp, will limit the compass of its music and mar its harmonies forever." It is of the utmost consequence, then, that you preserve a good conscience. It is your most important faculty. And yet it is exceedingly difficult to keep it from being led astray through ignorance, or by prejudice or passion. So tender and susceptible is it of impressions, that it has been educated to sanction somewhere or other every sin and crime that fills the pages of human guilt. It is impossible, therefore, to overstate the necessity of having a good conscience; a conscience enlightened by the word and spirit of God. For, unless our moral nature respond to our intellectual, our bosom is the seat of terrible war. There must be peace at home. The conscience must be satisfied with the choice of the profession we make, or we shall want moral courage for its prosecution. To undertake the pursuit of a business that our own heart is all the time telling us is wrong, is like a general marching an army into an enemy's country and leaving the fortresses and forces of his enemy unconquered in his rear. They will of course annoy him, cut off his supplies, and finally destroy him, unless he is able to turn upon them and crush them. But it is not every conscience that is a safe guide. An hour ago Saul of Tarsus had as clear a conscience that he was right when going to Damascus to persecute men and women unto death for being the followers of Jesus, as when he went to Cæsar's block to be beheaded for his faith in Jesus as the Son of God. The Jews did not know that Jesus was the Son of God and the Lord of glory when they crucified him. They put him to death with a good conscience, thinking they were serving God and their country; yet they did it with wicked hands. They committed an awful crime, though unconscious of it at the time. While, therefore, the conscience is not always to be trusted—for there is a blind conscience, an ignorant, unenlightened conscience—it becomes every one to try his conscience by prayer and by the Word of God, and be sure to have its approbation at the moment that he feels the eye of God beaming most fully upon him. And *again*—

Thirdly. Let a young man, in choosing his pursuit for life, examine carefully whether the business he is setting his heart upon inspires him with a *strength of will* to execute all the plans which are necessary to carry it out. It is folly to choose any calling that we have not courage to follow. So tremendous is the power of the will as an administrator of human affairs, that under God, and next to God, it is omnipotent. In debating in your own mind, then, whether or not you should choose this profession or that calling, strive to ascertain which one it is that inspires your soul with the greatest strength, and girds you up the most for difficulties and for victory. In relation to which pursuit of life do you feel that success is in you? As you look at its difficulties and dangers, and greatness, do you feel within yourself, God helping, that you have the elements of success within you?

One of our countrymen long devoted to our educational institutions, in describing the men we want in our day, said: "We want no men who will change like the vanes on our steeples, with the course of the popular wind; but we want men who, like mountains, will change the course of the winds." These are just the men wanted now: *men who, like mountains of granite, will change the course of the winds.* Men who are not at all distressed about the hosannah of the crowd; men who leave popularity for dolls, and remember, with an ancient, that the path of the gods is steep and craggy; men who are willing sometimes to go to Coventry, and let the populace howl on their coldest contempt; men who prefer the right to the greatest temporal advantage or honor; who can contest the frowns of fortune, and make good their course over the roughest seas. The ancients thought a virtuous man bearing misfortunes a far nobler sight than to see him basking in the sunshine. It is pleasant to see a clipper come flying into our glorious Gate with sails all set and colors flying; and yet, more heroic feelings are stirred within us when we see a noble vessel that has battled with winds and waves for six months, still making good her harbor, though some of her sails are torn and some of her masts shivered, and every timber in her has been tried by the tempest.

It is impossible to overestimate the importance of a rigid adherence to right principles where public sentiment is so fickle and yet so potential as with us. Public sentiment—the embodied opinions of the public—is like the atmosphere. It is sweet and fresh, pure and gentle, or hot and feverish, just as the breath that is breathed into it is hot or fresh. When it comes from the marsh or the fever-guarded district, it is sickly; but if from the lovely vale or the pure mountain heights, it is healthful. But when the hot sands and sulphurous blasts of the desert gather into the moving mass, then their course is marked with desolation. The particles of air and grains of sand are in themselves small and feeble. It is their *aggregation* that makes them powerful. It is the poison they gather in coming over the infected district, and the momentum they acquire in their progress, that make them so pernicious. And it is just so with public opinion. One man's calling, plans, thoughts and preferences by themselves may be so insignificant as to have but little influence; but when joined with those of his neighbors, they assume a shape and a weight that make them influential. There is then an individual responsibility resting on every one for his part of public sentiment. As threads make the web, so do individual opinions form public opinion. And when, as is sometimes the case, public opinion is wrong, then it is we are to show our attachment to our country and our adherence to principle, by maintaining the right, regardless of the fury of the storm. A time-serving trimmer deserves nothing but contempt. Let us know what a man really is, and then, even if we differ from him, still we respect his honesty and courage. We know where he is, and that he stands by his principles and is true to his flag; that he will not sail under false colors. But one says, it is of no use, because I cannot realize what I wish. The public are against me. I cannot resist the tempest. Now it may not be given ordinarily to one man, nor to any one age, or class of men, to mould public opinion all at once. It is usually the growth of many days, and the product of many minds; but still, an individual responsibility rests on every one for his part of it. Nor is it given to any one to know how great the effect may be of a single utterance of the right word, or of a good example, or of the lifting up of the right banner at the critical moment. The Rev. Dr. Wayland, of Rhode Island, holds some views that we cannot receive, yet we respect his character, and commend the following explanation of his success as an author, a teacher, and as a minister. It is reported that when asked how he had been able to do so much, and to live so long and so happily in the same community, he replied: "Whatever success I may have had in life, is owing simply to my holding on and sticking to my appropriate work." Yes, young gentlemen, this is just it. Hold on and hammer on, and look up, and never yield to difficul ties. Never think of giving up and lying down in despair. You may not be responsible for the storm; but you are responsible how you bear it—for holding to right principle—and so far at least, it is your duty to make a stand against the flood. There is nothing more sublime than honesty. Be sure, then, to ascertain what true principles are; and then hold on to them, come what may. In all your business transactions, whatever profession or calling you choose, let justice be your pole-star. The proverb, "Let justice be done, though the heavens fall," seems to imply a fallacy. For the more justice is done, the more the heavens will not fall. It is impossible for the heavens to fall, if justice is done. It is only by wrong doing the pillars of the skies can be shaken down. If then already, or even at the threshhold of life, you should find that you have made a mistake and chosen a calling that is not morally right, then you should leave it as quickly as you would leap from a vat of boiling brimstone, if you should fall into one, and be left with power to exert yourself to get out. If a barber should batter his razor's edge on a flint stone as a preparation for shaving, you would not be likely to trust yourself his hands. Why then will you risk wearing off or gaping or *dulling* your conscience by daily putting it into contact with known error, or moral wrong doing?

2. In the *second* place, allow me to say, some regard should be had to *your special qualifications for the pursuit in life which you are to follow.* The gifts which God bestows upon his creatures are indications of their sphere of existence. The fins and breathing apparatus of fish are adapted to the sea; and so the wings and shape of birds indicate that their home is in the air. And the human form and constitution clearly point out our adaptedness to the world in which we live; into which we have been born and out of which we are to die, when our course is finished. But we have a more specific adaptation than what is here indicated. God in all ages has endowed some men with special qualifications for certain pursuits. A careful study of history shows that all the ages of mankind are united as links in a chain; that all

generations of men, like the geological dynasties and periods of the planet, are connected together, and exert an influence upon and are preparatory to all that follow. Past generations lap over upon us, just as we will do upon the one that follows, and through it upon all that shall follow to the end of time. And so also different nations and races act upon one another, and each age of the world and each nation has had, and still has its peculiar, distinctive mission in the world to fulfil. And for its mission, providence allotted to it the proper gifts and opportunities. But again, this is true of individuals as well as of ages and nations. Cain was the first builder of cities, and from him we have our word civilization. Jabal was the leading agriculturist of h's age, being "the father of such as dwell in tents and have cattle," and his statue should therefore crown the entrance to our cattle-shows and agricultural fairs. And Jubal, his brother, was "the father of all such as handle the harp and the organ;" and his statue should therefore prevail over all the images of gods and goddesses of the heathen in our concert halls. And Tubal-Cain, the Vulcan of the Old Testament, should preside over the blacksmith and the whitesmith, and the goldsmith and the mechanic's hall, for he was the father of all the mechanics, "the instructor of every artificer in brass and iron." We are authorized also, by the word of God, to say that gifts and talents of men, by which they are adapted to the various employments of life, are imparted to them by the Creator. "There is a spirit in man; and the inspiration of the Almighty giveth him understanding." The classic page as well as the inspired writers tell us that God has taught man how to sow the wheat, thresh out the corn, and to get riches, and to fell the trees, and even how to fight. It was God that gave Moses administrative power, and to Aaron the gift of eloquence. Othniel, Samson, Gideon, and Daniel were raised up to be warriors; and so were Alexander the Great, Wellington, Napoleon, Havelock, and Jackson. And Cyrus was the Lord's anointed for the special purpose of delivering his church out of Babylon. "And the Lord spake unto Moses, saying, See, I have called by name Bezaleel the son of Uri, the son of Hur, of the tribe of Judah: and I have filled him with the spirit of God, in wisdom and in understanding, and in knowledge, and in all manner of workmanship: and I, behold I have given him Aholiab, the son of Ahishamach, of the tribe of Dan; and in the hearts of all that are wise-hearted I have put wisdom, that they make all that I have commanded thee." And so of statesmen, artists, orators and philosophers, they were specially blessed with the gifts or endowments that were fitted for the positions or works in life which they accomplished. Let every young man, therefore, carefully examine and see whether his mental and moral endowments fit him for the business he is about to choose, or whether, at least, he feels within himself that he has the capacity and the energy that will enable him to prepare himself for it. It is said in the Life of the late Moses Stuart, one of the best men and best scholars of our country and of our age, that the trustees of Andover elected him to a professorship, not because he was prepared, but because they were satisfied it was in him, and that he would thoroughly prepare himself for it. And nobly did he justify their confidence. Be sure, then, that you are fitted for the place, rather that it is merely for you.

3. In the *third* place, young men should consider it as a great principle to follow in choosing their occupation, *that it is one by which they may hope to be useful, to do good in the world.* Having determined that all men are not equally fitted for all pursuits, but that some are better qualified for one employment, and others for another, it is plainly the will of God that labor should be divided, and that the arts and pursuits of life should be so multiplied and meted out, that all should have something to do. The rule by which callings are graduated is not a rule to determine which are the highest or the lowest. It has reference only to two things, namely: that the calling is a righteous or lawful one in the sight of God, and that we have gifts from God for its prosecution. True honor lies in the manner of filling such a calling. No

matter what it is, if it is one that God approves of and has called us to; then, if we fill it well, it is honorable. One of our old divines has said, that if God were to commission two angels, the one to rule an empire and the other to sweep the streets of a city, both would proceed to their work with equal alacrity. As prejudice may exist in some minds simply from the want of clearly apprehending the distinction and relation that must exist between the different callings and employments of men, we have here a few words to say concerning them. *Art*, and the *Fine Arts*, and *Manufacturing*, are terms in everybody's mouth, and yet but few seem to see how they are united in concord. The lowest or simplest idea of manufacturing is suggested by the etymology of the word, which is from the Latin, and means " the making of anything by the hands;" that is, without the help of instruments or machines. And yet our manufactured wares and goods are almost all made in whole or in part by machinery. The literal signification is, therefore, so limited that it properly applies to but few things. For we have but few articles that have proceeded from the human hand only, acting mechanically; but the moment a directing intelligence is seen in the working of the hand, then we have *Art*. Hence we find in the books and in constant use the phrases, "the art of ship-building;" "an art in making tools, wagons and ploughs," and the like. And one step more, and we have the Fine Arts, namely, the pursuits of man in which his hand and his head and his heart are all working together. The hand is at the bottom and it is at the top of everything. Without manufacturing nothing is done; and without intelligence to direct the hand, nothing is done; and without taste, an enlightened heart, with the directing mind, there is no Fine Art. And as this triple group is combined to a greater or less degree in all our pursuits and enjoyments, and thus the whole man is consulted and honored, so it is with all the proper pursuits of mankind. They are all honorable and they are all united. The farmer has need of the merchant and banker, medical man and mechanic, and all these depend upon the farmer for their bread. The universal law is, I have need of you, and you have need of me.

But still the question is not answered: Is the young man to be a farmer, a mechanic, a merchant, a physician, a teacher, a lawyer, a sailor, a soldier, or a minister of the Gospel? All these employments and the multitudinous branches or modifications of them, that are too tedious to be enumerated, are lawful and morally right in the sight of God. The cultivation of the earth is, of course, the oldest pursuit of man, and its importance is obvious. All other professions and pursuits depend upon agriculture. The temporal wants of the world must be supplied. And here we notice a popular fallacy which has long occupied the minds of our countrymen. They have been disputing which was the greatest, "King Commerce," "King Gold," "King Cotton," or "King Labor," whereas, in fact, the true and mightiest king is BREAD. And while there are millions of mouths to be fed, and millions of acres that want hands to till them, it is clearly the will of heaven that millions of our race should find the pursuit in which they are to do the most good by toiling in the field. And of *mechanical industry*, we may say it is essentially connected with agriculture, because it lives upon the produce of the ground, and it gives the farmer his house and barns, mill and implements, and then it builds ships which the merchant employs in carrying the products of the farmer's lands from one country to another. And thus the farmer, mechanic and merchant are component parts of human society mutually or reciprocally dependent upon each other, and the banker is but another member of the same firm, and Providence indicates by gifts and resources which branches of this business each one is to pursue. The *medical profession* is ancient and honorable. The great Redeemer was a healer of the bodies of men as well as the Saviour of their souls. It is manifestly our duty to take care of the body. For sound health, and a body perfect in all its members, is necessary as an instrument for serving our fellow men. But few consider how much society owes to the medical profession. But few consider how much suffering they save us from, and how many lives they prolong and how much usefulness and happiness they produce in the world. The world is ungrateful to medical men. In learning, talents, diligence, science, self-denial, toil and usefulness, it is difficult to take too high a view of the professors of the healing art. But perhaps stronger prejudices exist against the *legal profession* than against the medical. But wherefore? It is not sinful, *per se*. It is impossible to think so, or to maintain any such an opinion. For God himself is a lawgiver and judge and a law executioner by his laws, which he has made to pervade everything. Does not the legal profession expound the principles of truth, and teach us what equity and justice are, and vindicate the rights and redress the wrongs of society? The history of the legal profession shows that human learning, science and liberty and civilization and of Christianity owe a great debt to its members. The profession of the law is indeed a noble one. Its true object is to promote what is just, equitable and right. Statute and civil law embrace a large portion of human history, and the common law has its deep foundation in man's moral nature, and regulates his whole ethical economy. If it is not always administered by able and true men, it is not for the want of a training, discipline and excitement that should produce such. And as a body, we believe, legal men are men of high principles, and the conservators of human rights and of eloquence and sound learning. But, perhaps, the work of the *teacher* is more important still. In all the other pursuits of men, the work is done with the materials furnished. In all other departments of human labor, even the office of the pulpit, the influence exerted is upon and through agencies that have been already developed, either physical, scientific, military, philosophical, political or literary; but it is the teacher's office to form the mind and the character—to prepare the instruments by which all the other pursuits of life are to be carried on. Thus it is the law of heaven that man's work should be *associative.* One man can neither build a navy nor carve a whole cathedral himself; but he can do his part, and when others do their part, and the results are associated, the work is done. And thus, also, the promotion of our own individual welfare is not only lawful, but a duty, when it does not interfere with our higher duties to God and our fellow-men. The true aim of all personal improvement should be the glory of God and the happiness of his creatures. For whatever is truly great in humanity is the expression of man's delight in God's work. It does not follow because a man is forced to mechanical labor for his bread, or to wear away his life in ceiled chambers behind a desk, or to dig his life out of dusty furrows, that he is cut off from the teachings of his Maker. But if a man allow his profession or occupation to lead him away from the Great Teacher, and blind his eyes to the splendor of his works, and bind up his life-blood from its beating responsively to the calls of his omnipotent love, then indeed he is blind and helpless and miserable. But it is not wrong—rather it is a man's duty to support his family, or to help his parents in old age, or to win a bride, or to endow a college by making money; but when at his work, or engaged in his profession, he should love, and love every touch and every blow and every step that it requires to make it square work, perfect work, finished work, such as the great Grand Master will accept. It is only when a man has an enthusiastic love for his calling, that the spirit is upon him, prompting him to its highest attainments. A love for one's calling is essential to success and happiness. Fame and money and position are proper objects to aim at in a subordinate degree. But the love of these things must never be the first motive in the choice of a profession. Mr. Ruskin, in one of his lectures on Art, lays down the rule for his pupils in this way: "Does your art lead you, or your gain lead you? You may like making money exceedingly; but if it come to a fair question whether you are to make five hundred pounds less by this business or to spoil your building, and you choose to spoil your work, there's an end of you. So you may be as thirsty for fame as a cricket is for cream; but if it come to a fair question, whether you are to please the mob, or do the thing as you know it ought to be done, and you can't do both, and choose to please the mob, it's all over with you; there's no hope for you; nothing that you can do will ever be worth a man's glance as he passes by. The test is absolute, inevitable—Is your art first with you?"*

It is essential, moreover, to this depth of feeling in one's profession, that it should be viewed in its relations to the works and laws of God as the Creator and governor of the universe, and that the mind should not be allowed to dwell on petty and mean cares. Things are very much as we conceive of them as to their effect upon us. Whatever business, therefore, you are to follow, do not let its little chagrins and disagreeable points fill your head. The constancy of small emotions will make your mind and heart little, if not mean. Strive to overcome all littleness, all jealousy and prejudice. Never mind what others think or say of

* Lecture on the Influence of the Imagination.

your calling, if you feel within yourself that it is right according to the will and providence of God. Keep your eyes and ears open, and your hands employed, and your mind quiet, peaceful, stayed upon God, so that you may forget yourself, and live out of yourself in your work, and in the calm and beauty, or grandeur and mightiness of God's great and lovely world. If there is grandeur in your own soul, you will see it outside of yourself, and find it in others also. Miracles only come to those who believe in miracles. The proverb says: "If you meet with no gods, it is because you harbor none."

It is then the law of God that man should labor, and labor under constraint of law. It is an error to say that we are born free, and that the fewer laws we are bound by, the fewer penalties we shall have to endure. This never was true. The laws of God are barriers to keep us from rushing over the precipice. It is only the lower animals that are comparatively exempt from laws. "No human being, however great or powerful, was ever so free as a fish. There is always something he must, or must not do; while the fish may do whatever he likes." Indeed, it is in man's moral restraint rather than in his liberty, that we see the grandeur of his nature. If the butterfly is more beautiful and free than the bee, still the bee is the more honorable, because it is the subject of laws. And so it is throughout the universe. . It is a compend, a code of laws, and the restraint of laws distinguish the higher and more noble creatures and things from those that are inferior. The archangel and the insect; the orbits and the oscillations of the heavenly bodies and the mote in the sunbeam; the power and glory of all things and creatures are in their obedience to law. The king of day has no liberty, but a dead leaf on the hill-side has much. The three talismanic words of national existence are LABOR, LAW, and COURAGE; or the plough, the restraint of laws, and the sword; so are they also the elements of individual strength and happiness. But as no true and lasting peace has ever been won by subterfuge, so there is no peace for you but that which you shall win over self, shame and sin.

It is altogether a mistake to talk of victory as a chance. There is no chance and no blanks in your history. All you have to secure is your own verdict for right doing, and you have your cause. Every work well done is a victory. And as gaslight is the best city police by night, so God has ordained laws for the universe, by which to protect it; for by these laws he brings to light and to a pitiless publicity, sooner or later, all wrong doing. The wages of sin is death. Darkness is the true friend of no man. For all sin, like murder, will out. And, moreover, by the very same laws, God has guaranteed that to the powers of sanctified intellect all recesses shall be opened, and all secrets revealed. Eternal sunshine glows around it. To it there is no height inaccessible, no depth that cannot be fathomed, no distance it cannot traverse. For all created things are governed by laws, and as far as we understand them so far the Creator invests us with his own attributes. It is by a knowledge of God's laws that we approach his attributes when we speak with the flaming tongue of lightning across a continent, or navigate our way through clouds and thick darkness, and contrary winds, to a desired port on the other side of the globe. Be assured then, young gentlemen, the conditions of life and death in yourself are the conditions of life and death in the nation of which you are a part. What is true here is true everywhere. Essentially the whole world and all its ages and races are alike. Do not deceive yourselves then with the idea that you may be advancing in unconscious ways to God and toward success. Do not go about to find an oracle or soothsayer to predict what you may become. You have it, each one of you has it in his power, at this very instant, to determine in what direction he will turn his steps, and what he will become, God helping him. Actions of resolute virtue are within the reach of every one of you. Honesty of purpose, singleness of mind, and steadfast devotion to a lawful patriotic business are within your reach, and challenge the admiration of mankind. And the best way of gaining strength of mind and elevation of purpose is to dwell long and fondly on, and ponder seriously on most worthy examples. As the prophet, by steadily gazing on the way by which his preceptor ascended to heaven, obtained his mantle, and a double portion of his spirit.

The GOSPEL MINISTRY is a profession of vaster scope and greater importance than any other. It must be so unless it is a gross imposture. If Christianity is what it claims to be, and the ministry of the word of reconciliation is a divine institution, then the preaching of the Gospel is the greatest work that can be committed to man. It is not necessary now to prove the divine origin of our holy religion, nor to show that God has a Church in the world having sacraments and ordinances, and an order of men called to preside in it, and administer its sacraments and expound the divine word to the people, showing them the way of salvation. The Apostle Paul has briefly stated the argument. The word is nigh thee; even the word of faith which we preach, namely, that if thou shalt confess with thy mouth the Lord Jesus, and shalt believe in thine heart that God hath raised him from the dead, thou shalt be saved. For with the heart, man believeth unto righteousness; and with the mouth confession is made unto salvation. For the Scripture saith, Whosoever believeth on him shall be saved.

How then shall they call on him in whom they have not believed? And how shall they believe in him of whom they have not heard? And how shall they hear without a preacher? And how shall they preach except they be sent? But the time does not allow us to dwell on the call and qualifications of the Gospel ministry.

4. Let me urge you, young men, in the next place, to endeavor most carefully to find out *the intimations of Providence* in regard *to the business you should follow.* I have reference here to your education, health, and place of residence. The influence of early training is felt and acknowledged by all. It was ascertained a few years ago, that out of one hundred and nine theological students, ninety-seven had either a pious father or mother, and eighty-eight had parents both of whom were pious. And the history of revivals of religion, and

even of conversions late in life, shows that they are almost all to be traced to early religious instruction. The seed grows after having long remained dormant. Samuel and Timothy, Augustin and Doddridge, are well known examples of parental piety giving shape to the character of their children.

General Jackson's rigid adherence to the articles of religion as a matter of faith—articles which he never allowed any one to dispute or ridicule in his presence without rebuke, is without doubt to be attributed to his mother's catechism and influence upon him in his earliest years. His affection for his wife and regard for her religious feelings are equalled only by the veneration he had for his mother. So strong were his convictions of the divinity of Christ and the inspiration of the Bible, that it was displeasing to him to hear them preached upon. He considered it useless to argue with a man that did not believe them. On one occasion at dinner with some British officers and others, one of his guests suggested that if we left the Bible out of the question he could prove his position to be true, upon which the old hero, bringing his hand down with considerable violence upon the table, said: "Never give up the Bible, sir, we can't give up the Bible." And General Havelock's whole religious character can be easily traced to the careful religious training of his mother during his infantile years—perhaps to the first six years of his life, while he was yet under his father's roof. It was his mother's custom to assemble her children regularly around her knees every day, and read a portion of the Bible to them, and pray with them, and explain religious matters to them. It was thus the English mother, in her humble house in Kent, was educating the British hero for Birmah, Affghanistan and India. It was there he learned those sterling principles that gave him strength for the day of trial. And at the first school he attended, so remarkable were his habits, that he was nicknamed "*old phlos*," that is, the philosopher. And at nine years we see "the man of fifty-seven through an inverted telescope." And, of course, you must consider your health and physical qualifications for the occupation you propose to follow. Health and capacity to labor and endure have a great deal to do with success in the world. A dumb man is not called to be an orator, nor is one of incurable stammering or of lungs so weak that he cannot engage in public speaking, called to be a lawyer or a preacher of the Gospel. The matter of health is too often overlooked. It is as much a sin to neglect the body as it is to neglect the heart. A spendthrift of health is a suicide where more than blood is spilt. For good health has a great deal to do with talents and success in life, and is not without its influence upon the realities of eternity. "Take," says one, "a lawyer's life through, and high health is at least equal to fifty per cent. more brain. The credit awarded to intellect is often due to digestion. Endurance, cheerfulness, wit, eloquence attain a force and splendor, with health, which they can never approach without it."

You must consider, also, the CIRCUMSTANCES of the place where you live. Such as to which calling or profession has the greatest opening for usefulness. Where your country has the greatest need of farmers, sailors, soldiers, mechanics, merchants, physicians, lawyers or ministers of the Gospel, and which calling or profession is the most crowded. As those born inland in farming districts are apt to become farmers, and those born on the seashore are more apt to become seafaring men, so you should consider whether your residence near an institution of learning and opportunities to obtain a liberal education, are not providential allotments, directing you to literary pursuits and some one of the learned professions. While one's youthful tastes or inclinations are not always infallible as to what kind of business is to be followed, still they should be most carefully considered. For, as the best medical treatment is to work with nature in her struggles to throw off ailments and overcome obstructions to her healthful functions, so as far as possible we should try by education and our daily pursuits to supplement nature, and help her to her highest aspirations. As our fallen nature is sinful, we must be careful how we yield ourselves to our natural preferences in choosing a business for life. That such youthful preferences are not always right, is clearly proven from the fact that they are not always successful, nor are they abiding. On the contrary, they are found to be spasmodic or fickle. A slight change of circumstances, or the flight of a few years, or the presence of a new acquaintance, or the absence of an old one, sometimes creates new tastes, or awakens just as strong preferences for another pursuit as were entertained a short time ago for a totally different one. Such preferences are often mere fancies. They are often delusions. The point should be decided upon principle. Numerous cases, and of distinguished men, too, could be given, in which it was found after years of trial, and a great loss of time and energy, that a mistake had been made in following these natural preferences in youth, and a radical change was made. There can be no doubt but that sometimes it is the duty of a man to change his business or his profession. This cannot be wrong in itself, but on the contrary, from health or other circumstances it may become a duty. A few years' experience may be necessary to develop what pursuit or kind of business we are the best fitted for. It is very evident either that some men have made a mistake in their calling, or else they are fit for no business at all. They are either in the wrong business or they do not attend to the right business in the right way, and in either case, the sooner they correct their mistakes the better for themselves and others. They are so fretful and unhappy, and attend to their calling so badly, that it is clear they are in the wrong place, or else not fitted for any place. Our doctrine on this subject is, that many men are attempting to do what Providence never called them to do, and that they ought to change either their calling or their manner of attending to it. For we hold that it is the duty of every Christian man and woman to strive to excel in whatever they profess to do. If a Christian woman has to nurse, or spin, or sew, or teach, the should aim at being the best nurse and the best worker. And if a Christian gains his liv ing by gardening or making boots, let him have the best vegetables and make the best boots in market. And so of every calling, from the humblest to the highest. That such should be our aim as a matter of policy and gain, may be taken for granted; but that is not enough. Christians are to covet earnestly the best gifts. It is their duty to seek superior excellence. They are to do more than publicans and sinners. And on this point, also, two remarks seem to be called for; *first*, as a general rule in *our* country, young people commence business or begin the duties of life too early. This has a serious and most baneful effect upon them in after life. It destroys the enthusiasm, cheerfulness and vigor that should uphold them in mature years. It is better that our boys live in less luxury, or even without some comforts at home, than that they should begin to make and spend money in their minority.

And *secondly*, it is a common fault in our day that our youth are so conceited, self-willed and obstinate, that they will not take the advice of parents, teachers, and friends of advanced years, as to what kind of business they should engage in. Parents, friends, and pastors may not always know "what manner of child this should be;" yet surely every young man should examine well his endowments and qualifications, and let the multitude of years speak to him, and age give him counsel, in deciding what business or profession his special gifts and circumstances may point out to him as his pursuit for life. Again, it will hardly be doubted that the *moral tendency* of the business we are deliberating about should be well considered; such as its liability to temptations to wrong doing, or its adaptation to promote our intellectual and spiritual improvement. We are not, indeed, to seek only our own interests; and yet we cannot help promoting our own highest good by choosing the right profession, and the right profession for us is the one in which we can get and do the most good. Some callings afford greater opportunities than others for reading, and others are more favorable for the development of the religious sentiment. For although the sweat of the man at the plough or at the anvil is just as honorable as the sweat of the lawyer at the bar, or of the statesman in the forum, still the ploughman and blacksmith have not the opportunities for mental cultivation that belong to the lawyer or senator. The toil of the merchant may be as honest, and as pious, and as acceptable to God as that of the pastor, but it is not so favorable for the genial studies and pursuits of cultivated minds. And it is no doubt because secular business, trade, and the learned professions are so engrossing that they do not allow or encourage that devotion to the culture of the mind and heart, that are requisite to eminence, that so few, comparatively so few are found earnestly pursuing secular avocations, that are at the same time eminent for their piety. Ordinarily eminent piety is preceded by, and still nurtured with much prayer and special attention to the reading of God's word. And this requires time and energy. And hence we should expect more piety, elevation of thought, and culture of intellectual powers in the ministry than in any other employment. As the subjects with which the teachers of Christianity are familiar are the most momentous that can occupy the human mind, so we naturally expect that a devotion to them would quicken and strengthen the intellect and improve the heart. The greatest enemies of human happiness are the trinity of human depravity: "the world, the flesh, and the devil." And it is perfectly clear that some callings are more beset by these than others. The love of ease is natural to the carnal mind. Sloth is a dangerous foe to all improvement. To hide our talent in a napkin is to betray our trust and dishonor our creation. And so also vanity and ambition, or the inordinate desire for fame, has slain its thousands. "How can you believe," said our Lord, "which seek honor one of another, and seek not the honor that cometh from God only?" Let not the wise man glory in his wisdom; neither let the mighty man glory in his might; let not the rich man glory in his riches; but let him that glorieth, glory in this that he understandeth and knoweth me, that I am the

Lord which exercise loving kindness, judgment, and righteousness, in the earth: for in these things I delight, saith the Lord. *Jeremiah* ix. 24.

The love of the things of this world grows by indulgence. The root of all evil is the love of money, "which while some coveted after, they have erred from the faith, and pierced themselves through with many sorrows." "They that will be rich, fall into a temptation and a snare, and into many hurtful and foolish lusts, which drown men in destruction and perdition." Observation fully confirms these texts of Scripture as to the blinding, absorbing, demoralizing, dangerous tendency of the inordinate love of the world. It is important, therefore, that a young man in choosing his business for life, and in the prosecution of it, should well consider the temptations it will present to him, and the hindrances that may be connected with it in the way of his mental and moral improvement. And the more so, because it is by these professional avenues, adaptations or peculiar tendencies that the evil one always makes his most deadly assaults. Is the calling, then, you are about to choose favorable or otherwise to your mental growth and spiritual welfare, or is it one that will deprive you of such advantages, and expose you to idleness, luxury or vice? Will it help or hinder you in your way to heaven? If then, as we have seen, our own personal well-being is not inconsistent with our duty to our fellow men and our Creator, but is a part of it, it must also be true that virtue should be its own reward, at least in part, in this world; and that we should seek for glory, honor, and immortality in the world to come. It is according to the Scriptures that we should have respect unto the recompense of rewards. Moses is commended for this. It is given as a proof of his heroic faith, that " he refused to be called the son of Pharaoh's daughter; choosing rather to suffer affliction with the people of God, than to enjoy the pleasures of sin for a season: esteeming the reproach of Christ greater riches than the treasures in Egypt: for he had respect unto the *recompense of the reward.*" Several points are revealed in the

Word of God as to the rewards of eternity, that should be well considered.

1. They are to be in proportion to the trials of this life. We understand our Lord to teach this principle when inculcating self-denial as at the very beginning of our discipleship. "If any man will come after me, let him deny himself, and take up his cross, and follow me. For whosoever will save his life shall lose it, and whosoever will lose his life shall find it. Then Peter said, Lo, we have left all and followed thee. And he said unto them, Verily, I say unto you, there is no man that hath left house, or parents, or brethren, or wife, or children, for the kingdom of God's sake, who shall not receive manifold more in this present time, and in the world to come life everlasting." And so Paul teaches, when he says: "For I reckon that the sufferings of this present time are not worthy to be compared with the glory that shall be revealed in us?" "Rejoice, inasmuch as ye are partakers of Christ's sufferings; that, when his glory shall be revealed, ye may be

glad also with exceeding joy." "A witness of the sufferings of Christ, and also a partaker of the glory that shall be revealed." "Yea, doubtless, and I count all things but loss for the excellency of the knowledge of Christ Jesus, my Lord; that I may know him, and the power of his resurrection, and the fellowship of his sufferings, being made conformable unto his death; if, by any means, I may attain unto the resurrection of the dead." The rule is, IF WE SUFFER WITH CHRIST WE SHALL REIGN WITH HIM. The enjoyment of heaven will be the more glorious because of the trials we pass through. "That the trial of your faith, being much more precious than of gold that perisheth, though it be tried with fire, would be found to praise, and honor, and glory at the appearing of Jesus Christ." "What are these which are arrayed in white robes? and whence came they? And he said unto me, These are they which came out of great tribulation, and have washed their robes, and made them white in the blood of the Lamb. Therefore are they before the throne of God, and serve him day and night in his temple: and he that sitteth on his throne shall dwell among them."

2. The rewards of eternity are to be *according to every man's labor done in the body.* This labor must be, however, from pure motives, from love to God and man. The love of Christ must constrain us to the consecration of ourselves to his cause. The great Calvin, in expounding the text: "They that be wise shall shine as the brightness of the firmament; and they that turn many to righteousness as the stars forever;" says it means, "that the sons of God who, being devoted entirely to God and ruled by the spirit of wisdom, point out the way of life to others, shall not only be saved themselves, but shall possess surpassing glory, far beyond anything which exists in this world. Hence we gather the nature of true wisdom to consist in submitting ourselves to God in simple teachableness, and in manifesting the additional quality of carefully promoting the salvation of our brethren." The rule is that in bestowing eternal life upon his followers, a

special reward is attached to special gifts and services. Our Lord accordingly promised to the apostles, in view of the extraordinary trials, sufferings and labors through which they were called to go, that they should "sit on twelve thrones judging the twelve tribes of Israel." Paul was, therefore, authorized to say, when he contemplated the end of his mortal race, conflict and labor here below: "Thenceforth there is laid up for me a crown of righteousness, which the Lord, the righteous judge, shall give me at that day: and not to me only, but unto all them also that love his appearing. The plain meaning of which is, that a special crown was prepared for him in proportion to his labors performed out of love to Christ. Paul, in his letter to the Corinthians (1 *Cor.* iii.), expressly tells us that, neither is he that planteth anything; neither he that watereth: but God that giveth the increase. Now he that planteth and he that watereth are one: *and every man shall receive his own reward according to his own labor.* And then he explains, that according to the character of a man's work, whether it be gold, silver, precious stones, or wood, hay, stubble—whether it abide the trial by fire, for the fire shall try every man's works of what sort it is—*so shall he receive a reward. And every man shall receive his own reward according to his own labor.* Not according to talents, gifts or station; not according even to our successors, but according to our labors, we are to be rewarded. Diversity of gifts in unity of purpose is God's law in all his works. Ministers and teachers and persons in all pursuits have different gifts, and different services to perform, and the rule by which they are to be rewarded at last, is according to their labor. It is a great comfort to see the fruit of our labors now, but if not, our record is on high. In one of the publications of the *A. S. S. Union*, there is an allegory to the following effect. We do not attempt to recite it word for word, but give an abridgment of it from one of the annual reports of the late Rev. Dr. Van Rensselaer, of the Board of Education, to the General Assembly. Indeed, we are indebted to this report for suggesting this discourse, and for many hints and thoughts, all of which we have freely used. The allegory is called "THE CROWN ROOM." A pious young man of promising talents and prospects felt impressed with the idea that it was his duty to preach the Gospel. He was exceedingly reluctant, however, to devote himself to the service of God in the Gospel of his Son. The struggle was continued for months. His worldly ambition and wealthy and fashionable friends pleading on the one side, and the voice of his soul seeming to rise up from its depths, saying, "Woe is me, woe is me, if I preach not the Gospel." At last he thought he had rightly settled the question. He determined not to preach the kingdom of God, engaged in business, and his immediate success he considered as a proof that he had done right. He soon became a man of large wealth. Nor did he forsake the cause of Christ. He maintained his Christian profession, and was punctual at the prayer meeting, and gave liberally at the missionary concerts. After being at a large meeting in behalf of missions, he returned home, and soon fell asleep, when he dreamed that an angel of great glory approached him and invited him to follow him. He did so until he reached the gate of a stupendous edifice. After entering its apartments, whose dimensions and magnificence amazed and awed him, "This," said his angel guide, "is the *Crown Room*, and here you see deposited the crowns which await the faithful when they have finished their course." And oh, what a sight was there presented to his eyes! Arranged in glittering rows, one above the other, suspended from the lofty dome and piled up on every side, were innumerable crowns of every size, form and device. Some of these were simple circlets or crescents of gold, containing here and there a single jewel; others more thickly sprinkled with brilliants or studded with gems. Long and earnestly did he look at the glories that surrounded him until his guiding angel reminded him that it was time to return, and began to move out, but said, "Thy crown is yet to be won." But being reluctant to leave, his eyes were at last fixed upon a crown which he had not before observed. It was gorgeous with brilliants, and as he gazed upon it a strange fascination seized him. He trembled as he gazed, and tears fell from his eyes as he exclaimed: O earth, earth! what canst thou offer like this? Tell me, oh, thou shining one! for what favored being can this glorious crown be reserved—who shall be worthy to wear it at last? "Alas! alas!" said the angel, "I know not! once, indeed, it seemed ready for thee, but thou knewest not the time of thy visitation. Thou didst turn away from yonder glittering crown. I know not who shall stand in thy lot, or wear that resplendent diadem!" Startled, he awoke from his slumbers. The scales fell from his eyes, and he saw how he had temporized with duty, and had offered *gold*, GOLD, GOLD instead of the living sacrifice. How he had allowed the pleasures and gains of earth to delude him. He struggled long and earnestly for forgiveness. He now prayed, not "I pray thee have me excused," but in the very words of our text, "Lord, what wilt thou have me to do?" "Here am I," said he, "send me now, O Lord, if thou canst after so much unworthiness and so great neglect of duty." Bitterly, most bitterly did he mourn over his folly and repent his waste of talents, loss of time and misuse of precious gifts. But at length, finding peace, and becoming assured that it was his duty to preach the Gospel, he took up his cross and went forth as Christ's ambassador. Domestic ties and many worldly cares were now a serious hindrance in his way, but by divine grace he was enabled to strive for the prize set before him, and to do a great and blessed work in the service of his gracious Master. *Young men*, let me beseech you to choose an occupation that will bear the scrutiny of the last day. Consider well the principles laid down and briefly alluded to or illustrated in this discourse. Your happiness now and through a boundless eternity, as well as that of those whose life and being may be bound up in yours, depends very much upon your making choice of the right kind of an employment or pursuit in life. Choose, then, your calling in the fear of God, and so pursue it as to show that you are called of God to it, and that in it you are seeking to please Him who is invisible, and to gain glory, honor and immortality in his presence. Make your choice deliberately and according to high and noble principles, and then pursue your employment boldly, conscientiously, devotedly, persistently. A wrong choice, or a negligent pursuit even of the right calling, is a life of monotony for your own souls, a palsy in your own homes, and a misfortune or an injustice to others; while, on the other side, he that is wise is wise not only for himself, but for others—a wise choice and a wise pursuit is the life of the crowned and reigning spirit. *Thy crown*, young man, *is yet to be won.* God help you to gird on your armor, and help you to win it. It is a resplendently glorious crown, to which your age, your country and your God calls you. It is for you to become a light always moving in the creation of God, in a wider and a higher sphere—discovering always, illuminating always, gaining every hour in strength for bolder and more lofty flights, yet bowed down every hour into deeper humility; sure of being always and irresistibly in an upward progress; happy in what you have achieved, happier still in the greatness of the way before you, and happiest still at the close of life, when all other names of dearest ties may fade from the memory, to be refreshed by the recollection of that name which is above every name, happiest at the close of life, when the right hand begins to forget its cunning, to remember that there was never a touch of your chisel or of your pen or pencil, nor a deed done by your hand, nor a purpose of your heart, but has added to the knowledge and happiness of your fellow-men.

XII.

RESPONSIBILITY FOR THE SALVATION OF OUR FELLOW MEN.

If thou forbear to deliver them that are drawn unto death, and those that are ready to be slain; If thou sayest, Behold we knew it not; doth not he that pondereth the heart consider it? and he that keepeth thy soul, doth not he know it? and shall not he render to every man according to his works?—Proverbs xxiv. 11, 12.

One of the best remarks of the late Daniel Webster is his answer to the question: What is the greatest subject a man can think upon? "His responsibility, his responsibility to God, sir, is the most important subject that can enter his mind."

We propose now, in a plain way, with God's help, to offer some thoughts upon our responsibility as Christians for the salvation of our fellow men. To understand this passage of Scripture, we must consider, *first*, the sin here declared to be so displeasing to God. It is a sin of *omission*. It is the neglecting of our duty toward our fellow men, and though originally applied to their natural lives, it is equally true as to neglecting their souls. The original allusion seems to be to the case of an innocent person brought into visible and extreme danger, either by severe oppression, or by a sudden assault upon his person, or by some unjust process of law. As for example, if a person is condemned by false witnesses, and it is within our power to furnish the proofs of the perjury of the witnesses and the innocence of the party accused, then it is our solemn duty to do it. Among the Jews, it was allowed that if any person could offer anything in favor of a prisoner, after sentence was passed, it was his duty to do so before the execution. According to the Mishna it was usual when a man was led to execution, for a crier to go before him and proclaim: "This man is now going to be executed for such a crime, and such and such are witnesses against him: Whoever knows him to be innocent, let him come forth and make it appear" Quoted by Dr. Doddridge.

It is admitted that if any one is attacked by force, and his property and life are in danger, it is our duty to fly to his assistance, if there is a greater probability that we can save his life than that we should lose our own in the attempt to save him. Thus, if we see any one through ignorance or thoughtlessness exposing himself to danger, or about to walk over a precipice, or to fall into the hands of thieves, or to take a wrong road, or get into any other distress, as strangers, travellers, and ships at sea, and all such cases; then, though it might be with expense, toil and trouble to ourselves, and even with great difficulty and peril, and without any reward or even return of gratitude, still it is our duty, because of the great bonds of human brotherhood, and for the love of God the great Father of mankind, to hasten to their help and deliverance. Among the Egyptians, "to be the accidental witness of an attempt to murder, without endeavoring to prevent it, was reckoned a capital offence, which could only be palliated by bringing proof of absolute inability to act. To be present when any one inflicted a personal injury on another without interfering, was tantamount to being a party to the evil done, and was punishable according to the extent of the assault."*

And if the neglecting of the natural lives and estates of our fellow men be so highly criminal, it must be much more heinous in the sight of God, to permit the ruin of their character, or the defamation of their families, or the perdition of their souls, without doing everything in our power to save them from being drawn unto death and slain by the sword of eternal justice.

Secondly. It is supposed in the text, that they who neglect to deliver those that are drawn unto death and are ready to be slain, are prompt to excuse themselves for this neglect. And this readiness to offer excuses is evidence, *first*, of a consciousness of guilt; and *secondly*, of having offered violence to the best feelings of human nature. For our first impulse on seeing distress, is to endeavor to relieve it. Our hearts then leap into our bosoms, and we are

---

* "Ancient Egypt," by the Carters, vol. 1., p. 80.

ready to run to their relief; but when cold and selfish calculation enters into the heart, then we forbear. And here is the force of the terms—*if thou forbear to deliver them*—that is, if thou check, or restrain, and hold back from doing what your heart prompts; then "he that pondereth the heart, and keepeth thy soul, doth not he know it? And shall he not render to every man according to his works?"

Thirdly. All such excuses, however, are vain. They are unavailing. If we succeed in excusing ourselves to ourselves and to our fellow men, it is a trifling matter. It is a light thing to be judged of man's judgment; he that judgeth thee is the Lord; and he pondereth the heart; he weighs in a most accurate balance, all its most secret sentiments. He that keepeth thy soul, doth he not know it? His are all thy ways, even to the deep thoughts of thine heart; and he will render to every man according to his works.

Human laws may not punish for the neglect of our own or of the souls of our fellow men. The grand jury may not bring in an indictment for profane swearing, or for drunkenness, nor for destroying the habits of our young men, or for adultery and fornication, and lying and corrupting our public morals. It may be the police cannot prevent men from exercising their ingenuity in decoying the innocent and deluding the unwary stranger. There may be no statute against the omission of duty to the souls of men. The laws of the land may not be able to punish for the sins of the heart, or to enforce filial piety and love to God, and charity to our fellow men, still he that trieth the reins of the heart, knoweth all these things. And besides, there is the common law of humanity, the written law of benevolence, engraved on the human heart and proclaimed from the statute book of heaven, requiring us to deliver those that are drawn unto death and are ready to be slain, and the supreme law-giver will render at last to every one according to his works.

The doctrine raised from this explanation of the text is, that THERE IS A GREAT RESPONSIBILITY RESTING UPON US TO DESIRE AND LABOR

EARNESTLY FOR THE SALVATION OF OUR FELLOW MEN. And this view of the text implies,

1. That our fellow men are in danger; and that the wicked, the impenitent, and ungodly are in a dangerous condition is clear from the Word of God. This danger is pointed to by the words: "If thou forbear to deliver them that are drawn unto death, and those that are ready to be slain."

Drawn unto death—ready to be slain, are fearful words. And all the more fearful when we remember that it is of the soul rather than of the body that they are spoken. Have you ever seriously considered what is meant by the slaying of the soul—by the death of the soul? What is the death of the soul? Is there, indeed, any reach of the human mind so capacious and all penetrating as to apprehend what it is to be lost? If eye hath not seen, nor ear heard, nor heart of man conceived, what are the joys of heaven: so neither hath eye seen, nor ear heard, nor heart of man conceived what is meant by the portion of the finally impenitent; the cup of trembling and wrath which an om nipotent hand compels them to drink, because they rejected offered mercy and despised the free grace of God. Weeping and wailing, and gnashing of teeth, and outer darkness and banishment from the presence and glory of God, are some of the terms by which the doom of the wicked is described in the holy Scriptures. But, oh, situation how dismal!

> "Dungeon horrible on all sides round
> As one great furnace flam'd, yet from those flames
> No light, but rather darkness visible
> Serv'd only to discover sights of woe,
> Regions of sorrow, doleful shades, where peace
> And rest can never dwell, hope never comes
> That comes to all; but torture without end
> Still rages, and a fiery deluge, fed
> With ever-burning sulphur unconsum'd."

And yet, is it not true that multitudes around us are living in sin and dying out of the present world every day without any preparation for a better life? Does not a thoughtful survey of our streets confirm the Scripture view, that the wide gate and the broad way which leads to death are crowded, and that there are but few in the narrow way which leads to life? Is it not true if we judge from our fellow-men at large as they pass and repass before us in their thousand thousand ways of conflict, suffering, living and dying, that Christ's flock is small and the devil's herd is large? If the destroying angel was commissioned to pass over the cities of christendom, and commanded to smite with instant death all those who dwell in houses not marked with the blood of the great Paschal Lamb slain from the foundation of the world to take away its sin, to slay the first-born of all those families that do not call upon God by morning and evening prayer—who do not reverence the holy name of the God of Israel—who do not keep his day holy, and who do not take up their cross and follow Christ—brethren, would not loud and long wailings rise up from many of our dwellings if such a test as this were now applied in order that it might be seen who is on the Lord's side and who is not? It is fearful to move over a field of battle, when the missiles of destruction are flying, rolling, rattling and crashing in every direction; or to go through a populous city when an epidemic is prevailing, and death rides on every breeze; but, there is no epidemic like sin. It kills both body and soul, and kills beyond the grave. There is no death like eternal death, which is the second death—a death forever in the extremest agonies of dying, and yet can never die. With all the allowances which that charity can make which believeth all things and hopeth all things, is it not true, that the marks of eternal death are on many of our fellow-men—that is, they are ungodly, impenitent, self-righteous, disobedient, utterly careless or indifferent about religion, or they are profane, prayerless, immoral, vicious? And on others on whom the marks of evil doing are not displayed, there are, however, no signs of spiritual life. They are not seeking to be saved. They are not given to prayer. They do not love God, nor obey his Son Jesus Christ. And if the righteous scarcely be saved, where shall the ungodly and the sinner appear? What shall be the end of those who know not God, and obey not the Gospel of his Son? O that the dreadful contagion of sin could be destroyed! But alas! it is an epidemic that rageth everywhere in our fallen world, and rageth evermore winter and summer, seed time and harvest. It never abates. Sin abounds and death reigns. "For death from sin, no power can separate." Now a few considerations will make it plain, that the impenitent are in danger of eternal death. *First*, they are in a great measure careless on the subject of religion. Intelligent, energetic, whole-hearted on all other subjects, they are indifferent to this the first and greatest concern of every human being. Their carelessness may arise from a variety of causes, but in every case it is dangerous. Some think themselves wise and increased in goods, while in fact they are stupid, ignorant and miserably poor. Their prosperity is either a mere fancy, or it is the verdure of the hill-side just below the volcanic crater, whose groanings are already to be heard as notes of preparation for the overflowing flood of fire that will sweep all below to destruction. They are sick, but think themselves in health. They will die, if no physician saves them; but they do not feel their need of one. Their carelessness is the calm that precedes the storm. It is a calm produced by ignorance or stupidity, if not by an entire withdrawing of divine influence. Indifferent, unconcerned, no mind or heart for eternal realities; how can they be saved? The Lord's day they do not keep holy. Their backs are turned upon the Lord's house, where his word is preached; and their Bible, the gift of a parent, or of a "sister dear" who has passed into the skies, if not lost, is at least not read; nor do they now repeat "Our Father" and lift up their hearts to God as they were taught to do in prayer in the home of their youth. How, then, can they be saved who neglect so great a salvation? Those who despised the law of Moses died without mercy; but to despise the Gospel is a greater crime, and deserves a greater punishment. Those who seek not mercy now, according to the Gospel, shall never have it. *This* is the acceptable time; *this* is the day of salvation. If it be neglected, there is then no more hope. But, *secondly*, our impenitent fellow-men are in great danger, because the manner of their lives is contrary to God's laws, and therefore exposes them continually to his righteous judgments. Some men are content with a mere name for decency and good manners; others are amiable and correct and well to do in the world; and others even have the form of godliness; and yet all these are without true piety. Some even draw nigh to God with their mouth, and honor him with their lips, whose heart is far from him. Then there are others who are living in open sin. They glory in their shame. Their sins are open beforehand, going before to the judgment, and some men's sins follow atter. The works of the flesh, which are the works of the wicked One, are manifest, which are " adultery, fornication, uncleanness, wrath, murder and drunkenness." And they that do such things show too clearly that they are of their father, the devil, and the lusts of their father they will do. They are servants of sin, and living after the flesh, they must die—*For the unrighteous cannot inherit the kingdom of God. Thirdly.* Another proof of the imminency of the danger that threatens our impenitent fellow men, is that great and fundamental errors are abroad in the world—and many are led away from the truth as it is in Jesus, and many even substitute these false doctrines and damnables heresies, as an apostle has called them, for the vital doctrines and true views of our holy religion. They receive *as* and *for* the precious Gospel of Christ, what is in fact another Gospel. The fancies and traditions and commandments of men are substituted for the commandments of the living God. A "will-worship" is put in the place of the worship God has appointed. Human means are made sufficient without the atonement of the Son of God. Now it cannot be true that all religions are equally good. It cannot be true that a man is not responsible for what he believes. It cannot be true that it makes no difference what a man believes if he is only sincere. If this were so, then there would be no difference between right and wrong. Nor could there be any standard of right and wrong. But we know there is such a difference, and that there is such a standard, and the proof of this is the universal conscience, confession and practice of the human race. And we know also that as a man thinketh in his heart, so is he. We know that truth apprehended is a principle, and that a principle apprehended excites an emotion, a desire, a will, and leads to action, so that from believing comes thinking, and then doing. Truth in itself is infinitely precious. It is separated by an infinite space from error. And while truth is saving, error is destroying. It does, therefore, make a great difference what a man believes, for without his intending it, or perceiv-it, his conduct is moulded by his belief. And besides, a man is as much accountable for the doctrines he believes, the sentiments he holds, the opinions he utters, as he is for the example he sets or the actions he performs. Nor does a man's good intentions excuse him for wrong doing, when he could have known what was right by taking heed to the will of God. Nor does a man's sincerity in his belief save him from responsibility. A man's sincere belief that his neighbor was honest does not save him from the loss he sustains when that neighbor runs away with his money. Nor does a man's perfect honesty save him from death, if by mistake he has taken poison that kills instead of the powder that was to heal. It is our duty to know and believe the truth, and nothing but the truth. And for this very purpose God has endowed us with reason, intellectual powers, speech and the means of knowledge, and has revealed his will for our salvation. It is by the truth we are begotten to a lively hope, and made free from sin. A man's life cannot be in the right, if his faith be in the wrong; for his conduct will flow from wrong motives and aims—his actions will be the products of erroneous principles, and however sincere, error never can produce right.

Since, therefore, it is philosophical as well as scriptural that some errors are "damnable," it is of the greatest importance that men should have clear and proper views of the divine character—of the law of God and of themselves—of its reach, spirituality and requirements, and of themselves as guilty in the sight of God, and of their need of Christ as a Saviour, and be able to apprehend his willingness and sufficiency as a Redeemer. And since, according to the Word of God, we cannot be saved without holiness—without being born again—without repentance and faith, and since so many are living around us who give no evidence of repentance toward God, nor of faith in Jesus Christ, is not the conclusion forced upon us, *they are drawn unto death, and are ready to be slain?* What becomes of the thousands of souls that leave our mortal shores every year? Whither do they go? What reasonable, scriptural hope is there that the majority of those who are now intent on gain or pleasure, and elbowing their way through our streets, will be saved when they die? Around how many of their dying couches will be gathered a praying band to commit the departing spirit to Jesus Christ? Ah! is it not enough that they die in wretchedness—that they die under the stare of strange faces, and among a people they have not known? Is it not enough that no mother, sister or wife will be there to watch their last moments with angel love, and when death has done its work, to close the eye and commit the body to dust—to strange dust, where sleep not the bones of fathers and their kindred? Is this all? Very far from it. This is only the death of the body. But—

> 'Tis not the *whole* of life to live,
>   Nor all of death to die;
> Beyond this vale of tears
>   There is a life above,
> Unmeasured by the flight of years,
>   And all that life is love.
> There is a death whose pang
>   Outlasts the fleeting breath;
> Oh, what eternal horrors hang
>   Around the second death!"

2. Let us consider next, *some of the excuses usually made or offered against our responsibility for the salvation of our fellow men.*

First. It is sometimes given as a reason for neglecting the spiritual welfare of those around us, that we do not know, and that indeed it is not our business to know anything of their spiritual state. Now, if by this is meant that every man must stand or fall before his own master: that every one has to appear before God for himself and not for another, and stand alone in the judgment as to his own individuality;—if by this is meant, that we are to mind our own business, and not meddle with the affairs of others, and that every one must work out his own salvation with fear and trembling, then it is all right. But if by this is really meant that we are ignorant of the dangerous condition of our impenitent fellow men, and that we are excused from feeling any anxiety or from doing anything to save their souls, then it is a wicked, atheistic, cruel fallacy, alike contrary to common charity and Gospel fraternity. *Do not know* that sinners against God are in danger of his judgments! And is it true, that you do not know that the wrath of God is revealed from heaven against all ungodliness and unrighteousness of men? Are not our fellow men out of Christ, living in sin, in the gall of bitterness and the bondage of iniquity, dead, absolutely dead in trespass and in sins? Do you not believe that all men are sinners against

God, and therefore children of wrath, and that, as the Scriptures say, we must be born again, become new creatures in Christ, and have a new heart, or we cannot see the kingdom of heaven? And are you not fully satisfied that human life is frail, short and uncertain; that ten thousand casualties and diseases are hurrying our fellow mortals to the gates of death and into an unchanging eternity? And does not the wrath of God abide on every unbeliever? Will he not render indignation and wrath, tribulation and anguish, upon every man who dies in his sins impenitent, unpardoned, unrenewed? Are not the wicked and all they that forget God to be turned into hell? Now, my brethren, do you not profess to receive the Scriptures as the Word of God? How, then, can you say you do not know the danger of your fellow men who are living in sin? Have you not yourself fled from the wrath to come, and do you not know that your friends who are yet living in sin are exposed to it? What would become of your friend, relative, child, or neighbor, who is now Christless, whose heart has not been renewed by the grace of God, if they should die this moment? Without repentance, must they not perish? Oh, say not, you know not their danger. Rather cry mightily to God that they may be saved, even as it were by pulling them out of the fire.

Second. Others say they do not feel the responsibility of which we are speaking, because they have their own affairs to attend to, and it is the minister's business to save the souls of men. Undoubtedly. It is true, you have your own souls to save and your own work to do, and it is the great business of ministers of the Gospel to labor to save the souls of men. They are set to watch for them as men that must give an account to God. But then have you no humanity? Are you without the milk of human kindness? Have you no sympathy, no fellow feeling for your own flesh and blood? It is the privilege and the duty of parents, sabbath-school teachers, and preachers, to show unto the people the way of salvation—to tell them what they must do to be saved—but does this excuse any of God's people from striving for the happiness of their fellow men? If our country is plunged into a war, and our coasts are to be defended against a foreign, invading foe, would it then be enough to say, let the officers of the government attend to our defence. They are the sons of the sword, let them fight for us. It is their business. True it is their business, but their duty does not excuse you from the claims of patriotism and honor. And what can the officers do without soldiers? They gain no victories with men of straw, nor with cork soldiers. It is theirs to plan, to lead, to command; but the bone and sinew, the hand and the heart of the soldier in the rank and file must be there to stand by the undaunted leader of the host, or all is lost. And just so it is with the ministers of the Gospel. They are God's servants, Christ's ambassadors; but they cannot do their own duty and that of the members of God's church also. Aaron and Hur must hold up Moses' hands while he prays, and Joshua leads the charge against the Amalekites. It is only thus the Philistines can be put to flight. The apostles were empowered to work miracles and to speak with tongues, and inspired to preach and write by the Holy Spirit, yet we find them, and particularly Paul, the bravest and the most learned, most eloquent and intellectual one among them all, repeatedly and most earnestly asking the prayers of the Christian Churches. Should you not then pray for your pastor, look over his failings, "to his faults be a little blind," and love and obey him? If you sincerely desire to remember his words, to profit by his instructions, you must pray for him and be a co-worker with him.

Third. Others say, we are commanded not to *cast our pearls before swine*, and therefore we must just let our fellow men alone in their sins. And has the devil become a Bible colporteur? Do I see him carrying his green bag of books, and quoting the sacred Scriptures? This is not at all improbable. He quoted the Bible in his temptation of our Lord in the wilderness, and our Lord conquered by quoting Scripture texts. The devil quoted to pervert and lead astray; our Lord quoted to correct his wicked perversions, and to vindicate the ways of God. It is true that some men do more harm than good by being imprudent. Their words are not fitly chosen, or the time and place were not wisely selected. There is a zeal that is not according to knowledge. It is possible to be overmuch zealous. New wine is not to be put into old bottles. The children of the bride chamber are not to fast while the bridegroom is with them. There must be moderation, and some attention to what is fit and becoming in times and places, characters and circumstances. But what miserable logic have we fallen on? Because a man may be imprudent, therefore he cannot be prudent. Because a man may be righteous over much, therefore, he must have no zeal at all. It is just the same logic that Milton puts into Eve's mouth, when she proposes to Adam to kill themselves to keep from dying. It is as practicable a method of doing our duty, as if we should say, it is possible we may be choked to death by eating, therefore, we will starve to death. Our Lord does indeed tell us not to cast our pearls before swine. Are all impenitent men, therefore, swine? Is there no way to administer reproof for sin? The Saviour's admonition implies that there is a prudent way by which to win the souls of men, and hence He warns us against defeating our purposes, and bringing upon ourselves contempt by injudicious attempts. There is an officious pietism, a cant—a long-faced whining and praying in the streets, and intruding evangelical tracts and conversation upon travellers, and even into people's houses, that is certainly unbecoming and highly injurious; but surely it does not follow, because of such ignorant and rude abuses, that we should all sit still, and see our fellow men drawn unto death and ready to be slain, and do nothing to save them. Was it not Judas, who said, what is that to us? And was it not Cain, who said: *Am I my brother's keeper?* Away with all companionship with such cruelties, away with such miserable sophistry as this, which the devil puts into men's heads to the everlasting undoing of multitudes of precious souls!

Fourth. Others say, our fellow men are able

to take care of themselves, they have the means of grace—the Lord's day, the church and the minister, an open Bible, as good an education as we have—they are free agents—they know their duty; let them attend to their own souls, why should we trouble ourselves about them? And truly it is a blessed thing to live in our day—to have the mantle of Puritan, Huguenot and Covenanter sires, who were the elect of heaven to preach the Gospel on this continent, and make the wilderness vocal with the worship of God. It is a great privilege to have ministers of the Gospel among us, who show unto men the way of salvation. It is, indeed, our crowning excellence, that we have houses of worship and schools for all sorts of children, and that the word of God runs swiftly over the land, and the printing press is casting the fruits of the tree of life abroad over all continents, and that a greater and a more decided Christian influence prevails over mankind than ever before since the foundation of the world, but still all these privileges do not excuse God's people from personal anxiety and efforts to advance his kingdom in the world. The mere letter of the Gospel does not convert and save. It is not by might nor by power, saith God, but by my spirit that men are converted and saved. And God's spirit is given in answer to prayer. His well-beloved son is to ask him for the heathen, and then he gives the uttermost parts of the earth to him for a possession. And, besides, it is well known that those who are most in need of the saving power of the Gospel do not themselves feel the need of it. They are dying for the want of bread, but have no appetite. Dying for the water of life, but have no thirst for it. They must be assisted, or they will never get into the pool when the waters are troubled. They must be encouraged or even led to the house of God or they will never hear the words of everlasting truth. It is known historically that savage nations are never civilized by an indigenous outgrowth. It has always been the result of something introduced from abroad. The germ of their civilization has always been planted among them by somebody else. It is philosophical that it should be so, for the stream cannot rise higher than the fountain. Like begets like. The earth is of the earth, *earthy*. It is then most clearly our duty, if God, for Christ's sake, has opened our eyes, to pray to him to open the eyes of our fellow men, and to endeavor to get them in the way that is most likely to prove availing to them for such a blessing. It is plainly our duty to furnish places of worship and the means of Christian instruction to all our fellow men, and then to do all we can to induce them to profit by such opportunities. If, by any fatal depravity, our fellow-citizens were so obstinate that they would sit in their counting-houses or stores, or starve to death in their parlors rather than procure and take their daily bread, would it not be charitable in us to supply them, and to persuade them to take it until they should so far recover as to know its value and seek it for themselves? Is it not within the prudent, modest reach of the influence of every one of you to induce a companion or acquaintance who does not now attend to religious things, to go to church and to keep the Lord's day holy? Is it not within the proper sphere of every one of you to bring some one to the Sunday school, the prayer meeting or the solemn assembly of God's people on the Sabbath? One word, one page, one prayer, one effort, with God's blessing, might be the means of saving many souls from death.

And after all, my brethren, is it not to be feared that the true reason of our neglecting the souls of our fellow men is, that we do not *realize* the importance of salvation—we do not really feel enough for their souls—we do not sufficiently realize spiritual and eternal things —we do not apprehend the greatness of salvation, nor the preciousness of the blood of Christ. If we only apprehended what it is to be saved, or what it is to be lost, then surely we should do more to deliver the souls of men from death. And the main reason why we do not realize these stupendous things is the want of faith. We want more depth of feeling, because we are ignorant and unbelieving. We have not a deep feeling for our fellow men because we do not truly believe what the Word of God says, nor do we pray for them, and love their souls as we should do, considering that we are redeemed by the blood of the Son of God.

3. *A few reasons why we should earnestly strive to deliver our fellow men from death.*

First. Our own experience should teach us to have compassion on the souls of others. Were we not in the same state by nature children of wrath even as others? Were we not on the very brink of destruction, when sovereign mercy found us; and shall we not seek to extend that mercy to others? We have found him of whom Moses in the law and the prophets did write, and shall we not invite others to come and behold him. We have looked to Jesus that we might live; and shall we not point others to the Lamb of God that taketh away the sins of the world? We have tasted that the Lord is good and gracious; and shall we not desire that all about us may have the same happy experience of his grace? We have obtained the forgiveness of sin through faith in his name; and shall we not, like David, endeavor to teach transgressors his ways? Oh, shall we not love the souls of others, as God, for Christ's sake, hath loved us—shall we not have compassion on our fellow-servants, as the Lord continually hath pity on us?

Second. We are so constituted that we have much INFLUENCE UPON OUR FELLOW MEN. None of us can live to ourselves. Each one has a share of influence. All covet influence, and yet but few realize what it is to be a man of influence. So great, indeed, is the influence of mind upon mind, of heart upon heart, that it requires much zeal and prayer on our part for our neighbor, lest we be guilty of neglecting his soul. "Be ye not partakers of other men's sins." If we forbear to deliver them that are drawn unto death and those that are ready to be slain—are we not partakers in their ruin?

Third. We should earnestly strive to save the souls of our fellow men, who are drawn unto death and ready to be slain, because when they are converted to God, *they are made happy.* The pleasures of religion are great both objectively and subjectively. The pious are not only saved from the wrath to come, but they enjoy at present in the life that now is, a good hope through grace and the sense of pardoned sin, a persuasion of the favor of God toward them, a belief that all things are working together for their good, and that when they die they shall go to heaven; and besides, the pious find great delight in prayer and praise, in hearing and reading the Word of God, and in conversation with religious people. These are joys that satisfy and sanctify the mind, and, compared to which, all the frothy mirth and carnal pleasures of the wicked are mean as the toys of children, and hurtful as the sports of madmen.

> "The men of grace have found
> Glory begun below,
> Celestial fruits on earthly ground
> From faith and hope may grow."

Wisdom's ways are ways of pleasantness and all her paths are paths of peace. Not a few have tried both the pleasures of sin and the pleasures of religion, and have found that there is more happiness in one hour's communion with God, than in days and months of sinful indulgence. The love of God is shed abroad in their hearts, which is unspeakable and full of glory. And the end of their faith is salvation—the joys and glories of the heavenly world. The Holy Scriptures teach us that Christ is gone to heaven to prepare mansions for his followers—that he will come again and take them to dwell with him where he is. The pure in heart shall see God. Verily there is a reward for the righteous.

Fourth. We should earnestly desire and labor for the salvation of our fellow men, because thereby we shall promote our own present and future happiness, the good order and peace of society, and the glory of God. Christians are the salt of the earth. Ten righteous men would have saved Sodom; and, verily, except the Lord had left us a seed, we had been as Sodom, and been made like unto Gomorrah. The prayers of the pious are a greater defence to their country than all its fleets and armies— and that government is most likely to flourish in which the people of God are the most numerous, and where truth and righteousness most abound. As the meanest service we can do for Christ has great refreshment in it, so whatever we can do for the souls of men from the love of God in our own hearts, increases our own happiness. Whatever is done unto one of the least of his disciples is done unto himself. They that be wise shall shine as the brightness of the firmament, and they that turn many to righteousness as the stars forever and ever. Our blessed Lord sendeth us not on a warfare at our own charge; not that we can do anything to bring God under obligations to reward us; for all we are is of free grace; and after we have done all, we are poor, unprofitable servants. Still it is a great honor to be the instrument of saving others. Such is the economy of grace, that in doing good to others, we ourselves are blessed. He that watereth the souls of others shall himself be watered. It is a glorious privilege to be made the means of bringing in a revenue to God's glory, year after year, and age after age. A good impression made in the Sabbath school, the influence of a single word, or prayer, or tract, or the education of a single youth, or the sending out of a single missionary, and thus to preach Christ by proxy, may be the means of bringing in a harvest of souls every year to the end of time. Herein is our highest honor, that we are co-workers with God and made like our merciful Father, who bestoweth his gifts upon us.

What can we do to save our fellow men? We should cherish a deep and ardent love for their souls; we should set them an example of faith and holiness, and invite them to the house of God; provide places of worship for them, that they may have no excuse; we should pray fervently for their conversion; Paul may plant and Apollos water, but God giveth the increase. The love of our neighbors requires that we should pity and help them in time of sickness, in poverty or other temporal distress; how much more, then, should we care for their souls and labor earnestly to prevent their eternal ruin! Solicitude for the health of their bodies and the well-being of their families and estates is esteemed friendship and love toward our fellow men; how much more, then, infinitely more, should we care for their souls; for what is time and all its multitudinous cares to that vast abyss of eternity, "whose end no eye can reach?" For what is a man profited if he shall gain the whole world and lose his own soul? or what shall a man give in exchange for his soul? *Matthew* xvi. 26. It were exceedingly important in such a city as ours, and in all new countries, and among all classes and assemblages of men who are from home or cut off from the enjoyments of social and domestic life, that the influence of our social nature could be secured on the side of virtue and religion. Much good and much evil is done by example, by conversation and by throwing newspapers, tracts and books in one another's way. One moment's reading while waiting in the parlor for the appearance of the friend called upon, or one sight of a picture, or one evening at a play or at the house of God, may fix the whole future character and eternal destiny of a young man or young woman. And if the children of the world are gregarious, and invite and even drag each other into the drinking saloon and to the theatre and to the chambers of pollution and death; how much more should Christian young men deliver them that are drawn unto death and ready to be slain! Perhaps no one thing destroys more men, especially young men, in our large towns and newly settled States, and in our army and navy, than the want of proper female society. Permanent resident families are few in comparison with the mass, and they are from different parts of the world, and are engrossed with their own social circles, and indifferent about widening them, and, consequently, husbands, brothers and sons *away from home,* in such a community have but few of the enjoyments of proper society. They seldom have opportunities to enjoy such refined delights, or to be strengthened in their purposes of well-doing by the restraints of sisters and mothers and pious female friends. Oh, it is greatly to be desired among us, that the hallowed influences of home should be thrown once more around the masses of men that are digging in our mountains, toiling in our valleys, or elbowing each other sharply through our streets and our crowded saloons.

REFLECTIONS.

First. Have we ever thoughtfully considered what is meant by the death of an immortal soul? Do we believe in its annihilation, or the destruction of its faculties, or the weakening or stupefying of its sensibilities? No. The death of the soul is its separation from the delights of the pious, from the joys of heaven, the raptures of redeeming love, and from the favor of God, its eternal Father. And what is more, the death of the soul is not only the loss, the unspeakable loss of God and heaven and all that makes heaven, but it is to be shut up in hell, with ghosts and damned spirits scratched and scarred with the thunderbolts of omnipotent vengeance. To be excluded from heaven is to be cast into hell. To be driven from the glory of God is to have his wrath poured upon the soul; and this is its death—woe, positive, lasting, deathless. But few of us desire to see, or can bear to witness one of our fellow men die as a terror to evil doers by the hand of the lawful executioner. Even where the method and instrument of execution are as kind and gentle as human ingenuity can make them, still the spectacle is tragical—so tragical that I am persuaded it would rend many of you to the heart to see one of your number dragged out into the street and executed on the scaffold or under the guillotine. But what would this deplorable circumstance be in comparison to the destruction of the soul! How much more deeply would it pierce your very souls to see the impenitent—however nearly related or by whom begot it will not avail—to see them led forth to that last dreadful execution, when Christ shall say: "As for these, mine enemies, who would not that I should reign over them, bring them forth and slay them before me." Then will begin cries and wailings that shall never end! Truly, as the apostle says, "He that shall turn a sinner from the error of his ways shall save a soul from death."

Second. Should it not excite us to more fervent prayer and to greater exertions to save our fellow men, when we reflect that if they perish they perish after the most precious provisions have been made for their salvation? Every possible means has been taken to prevent their death. There is balm in Gilead. There is a kind and an almighty physician there. We have the glorious Gospel of the blessed God offering pardon and peace to all men. The glad tidings of liberty are proclaimed to the captive. Health is offered to the sick; life to the dying. God so loved the world, that he gave his only begotton Son that whosoever believeth on him should not perish, but have everlasting life. Alas! alas! that men should be so stupid as to choose death when life is freely offered. Truly the ox knoweth its owner, and the ass his master's crib, but my people, with God, doth not know, doth not consider. Alas! that our fellow men should so shamefully reject the messages of eternal love, and obstinately refuse to believe on the Son of God. The consequences of this rejection is that they shall not see life, but the wrath of God abideth on them. Fearfully great must be the depravity of that heart that perverts all the means of grace into the savor of death. How melancholy it is that immortal souls should die under the Gospel! that they should abuse privileges so great and cut themselves off from the mercy of God! Verily, it shall be more tolerable for Tyre and Sidon, for Sodom and Gomorrah in the day of judgment than for the impenitent from Gospel lands.

Third. I am persuaded that it is so cruel and narrow, pitiable and mean a plea—"that it is nothing to you that others are in danger"— that none of you intend seriously to put it forth in abatement of your responsibility. It is one of the noblest feelings known to the human breast, that, in some measure, we are our brother's keeper—that his happiness is in part in our hands, and ours in his. A generous sympathy that makes heart throb responsive to heart, as shoulder to shoulder we toil up the hill bearing the burdens of life, marks heaven's true nobleman. If the people shall curse him who withholds corn in time of famine, shall not they curse him who withholds the bread of life from the famishing, and the cup of the wine of consolation from the dying, the water of life from lips parched with the fever of sin, and "goodness from such as are bound in affliction and iron?" Yea, God himself will send a curse, the bitter curse of Meroz, on all who come not to the help of the Lord against the mighty.

Fourth. Are we all conscientiously engaged in trying to deliver those who are drawn unto death and are ready to be slain? God alone can give a new heart to our fellow men; but we know also that the effectual fervent prayer of the righteous availeth much. Our heavenly Father is a God who heareth prayer. He is overcome by the importunities of his people. He is prevailed upon by the urgencies of the house of Israel. Are you then a husband or a wife, whose bosom companion knows not the Lord? If so, cease not to pray for him or her, with that humble confidence that is given to the Christian as he comes to the mercy seat. And, if you are a parent having an ungodly, a far wandered and prodigal child, then, like God's friend, Abraham, cry mightily unto Him, saying, *O that Ishmael might live before thee!* or like the father in the Gospel, Lord, have mercy upon my son. Offer prayer in secret, in the house of God, and in the family. Of Abraham, God says to his commendation: "I know him that he will command his children, and his household after him." And of Job, it is said, he rose early in the morning and offered up ten offerings for his ten children; because he feared they had sinned against God in their feasts with each other. He cannot love the souls of his family and fellow men much, who does not pray for them.

Our subject addresses itself with peculiar force to men of influence and distinction, to heads of business houses, officers of the army and navy, commanders of ships, employers of others, and parents and teachers, editors and publishers, and all who from any cause are heads of the people, and leaders of others. It is a fearful thing to live; but to live under obligations to be useful—to live in such a city as this—to live where you must be active in laying the foundations of the state and of the church, which are to be a blessing or a curse for generations to come—to live and set an example, and be responsible for such influences, is a fearful trust. Has God given you wealth, or genius, or position? And are you using your influence to deliver those that are drawn unto death and ready to be slain? Are you doing all you can to diffuse useful knowledge, and suppress intemperance and vice, and to elevate and purify public sentiment, to promote the right and prevent the wrong, and to bring your fellow men to a knowledge of the truth which is in order to salvation? Are you doing as you would that others should do to you? Young men and women are around you upon whom you can exert an influence for good—are you doing so? Suppose your sons and daughters away from home, situated as many of these are that we see among us, and what would you not give to secure for them the example and the prayers, and the counsels and the restraints of honest, sober, praying, Christian people?

How much it would gladden your heart to know that the people of God, in a distant city, were throwing around your children there the softening and elevating influences of the family circle and of good libraries, and leading them to the house of prayer and praise! Shall we not then do for the young people among us, as we would that the Christians of another city should do for our sons and daughters? As good citizens are we not bound to set a good example, and to deliver from death those that are drawn unto it by ignorance or intemperance, or evil companions, or any other wrong thing? And let us remember that what we do must be done quickly, for we are swiftly passing away. The season of harvest is short, and when it is past it is gone forever. I ask you, therefore, upon your conscience, and as you shall answer upon a dying bed, and at the judgment seat, are you doing all you can to deliver those that are drawn unto death and ready to be slain? But let all impenitent men know, that, however short of duty the members of the church may fall, still the condemnation of their unbelief will rest upon their own heads. Every one must give an account to God for himself. There is zeal enough in the church, and piety enough among its members, to be witnesses for God that religion is a reality. A thousand times has the conscience of the ungodly man told him of a truth, God is among these people. Ten thousand times has he felt the influence of their example, and the power of their prayers, when he neither knew nor acknowledged it. Nor will it at all mitigate the doom of the impenitent to know that the church failed in much of its duty. They themselves knew their duty, and did it not, and though there is censure upon the church, still their condemnation is that they would not accept of Christ; they would not come to Him that they might have life. If some are deluded; if some are hypocrites; if some are unfeeling and rude: still the question for the impenitent soul at the judgment seat will not be concerning the conduct of Christian professors, but what has he himself done in regard to this great salvation? May Almighty God, of his infinite mercy, grant you repentance unto life, through our Lord Jesus Christ, to whom be glory for ever and ever. Amen.

XIII.

THE PIETY AND PATRIOTISM OF PRAYING FOR OUR RULERS.*

HOLDING with the Catechism, and according to the interpretation of almost all commentators, Jewish, Catholic and Protestant, ancient and modern, that the "Fifth Commandment requireth the preserving the honor and performing the duties belonging to every one in their several places and relations, as superiors, inferiors, or equals," we design this morning to dwell on the *Christian duty and patriotism of praying for our civil rulers.* Our last discourse of this series was on the duty of children to parents. In the present we shall confine ourselves to one branch of the duty required of us

---

* This chapter is abridged from a discourse preached as pastor in 1813, in New Orleans, to the First Presbyterian Church and congregation of that city, and published by them. It was then widely circulated, but is now out of print. Only a few sentences referring to passing and local matters have been changed or omitted.

toward our superiors. The precept that requires us to obey and honor our *natural* parents is so broad and comprehensive, spiritual and dynastic in its reach, that it requires us also to honor and obey our *spiritual* fathers, and our *economical*, that is, our social and domestic fathers; and to honor and obey our *political* fathers. The duty which, however, we are now seeking to illustrate and enforce, is plainly taught by the apostles, and is specifically the duty of *praying for our civil rulers*. And we take our text for this subject from Paul:

I exhort, therefore, that, first of all, supplications, prayers, intercessions, and giving of thanks be made for all men: for kings and for all that are in authority; that we may lead a quiet and peaceful life in all godliness and honesty. For this is good and acceptable in the sight of God our Saviour; who will have all men to be saved, and to come unto the knowledge of the truth.—1 Timothy, ii. 1–4.

In these words of the great apostle to the Gentiles we have a DUTY ENJOINED AND THE REASONS GIVEN.

The duty is to offer prayer for all men, for kings and for all that are in authority. The relation of subject and magistrate resembles very much in kind, if not in degree, the relation of child and parent. The very same reasons in part, which bind the child to reverence and obey the parent, bind the subject to obey and pray for the magistrate. It is certainly true that the duty of praying for our rulers, implies the duty of praying for all properly constituted authorities in the church and the world—parents, teachers, legislators, judges, officers of the army and the navy—and for all that are possessed of wealth, learning or talent, or any other consideration that gives them influence among their fellow men.

The reason given for enforcing the duty is very similar to the reason given for obeying our parents—temporal as well as spiritual blessings are promised. First, that we may lead a quiet and peaceable life in all godliness and honesty.

Secondly, for this is good and acceptable in the sight of God our Saviour. To offer prayer for constituted authorities is good in itself, because it is useful to ourselves and to the public, and it is acceptable, accompanied with a godly life, in the sight of God our Saviour. This is the highest of all sanctions; and what is well-pleasing to God, is the supreme good and happiness of man. Duty and interest are always united.

A third reason is the encouragement offered: That God *will have all men to be saved and to come unto the knowledge of the truth.* That is, *God is no respecter of persons: but in every nation he that feareth him and worketh righteousness, is accepted with him.*

Divine mercy is offered alike to the beggar and the prince, to the slave and to the master, to all without money and without price. And since salvation is offered to all, that some of all classes—every one that repents and believes—may be saved; therefore, God wills that the Gospel should be preached to every creature, and that all men should be the subjects of our prayers.

It is here assumed, there is a God who is the

Supreme Governor of the universe; that prayer is instrumental in procuring his blessings; that our forefathers were men of prayer. Their school-houses, judicial benches and legislative halls, and battle-fields, were consecrated with prayer. It is assumed, also, that what Cicero and Montesquieu call virtue, but what Bible-taught politicians call religion, is essential to the well-being of society. Religion and virtue are, indeed, the main pillars and foundation of public peace and prosperity. If any doubt on this point, let them read, not the rantings of a bigot, nor the superfluities of a schoolman, nor the harangues of political clergymen, but the " Vindication of Natural Society," and " Reflections on the Revolution in France," by Edmund Burke, and doubt no more.*

And it is here assumed that civil government is necessary to the welfare of society; that it is the guardian of the public peace, and the security of every man's person, property and privi-

* These papers are as remarkable for philosophical acumen, profound research, extensive and minute knowledge, as they are for eloquence. See the Works of Edmund Burke.

leges. It is by the exercise of civil authority that we are secured in our civil rights, public interests and domestic institutions. But my chief purpose is to insist upon *the Christian duty of praying for civil magistrates.*

Whether phrenology or animal magnetism can account for it or not, it is certainly true that man is prone to go from one extreme to another. The safe medium he is rarely content to observe. Wherever the Church and the State have been united, manifold evils have resulted, alike disastrous to civil liberty and ecclesiastical purity. And on the other hand, where the Church has been happily freed from the trammels of State, there pious men seem to have ceased to feel sufficient interest in the State, they have given up the management of political affairs too much to the ungodly, and the members of Christian churches have not looked for sound principles in the men seeking their suffrages, nor have they sought, as was their duty, the divine blessing upon their rulers. It is not agreeable to a pious man to forego the quietness of his home and the devotions of the altar, and bear the heat and burden of political strife, yet some should certainly be found of self-denial and grace enough to engage in political life, and still preserve their Christian character above suspicion. From our practice, it would seem that when we are not compelled by law to pray for our rulers, then we consider ourselves released from all moral obligations to do so. But the very reverse should be the effect of such liberty on the heart of an enlightened, patriotic and pious citizen. As prayer must in its very nature be a free offering of the desires of the heart, to God; so the more free we are from legal coercion or restraint as to our religious duties, the more fervent and frequent should our prayers be in behalf of our government. And yet it must be confessed, the tendency of things among us, has been to neglect this plain duty. As since the Revolution we have not been required by law to pray for the king, and all the "Royal Family," so we have neglected to pray for the President and those in authority over us. But it is not true that this neglect is because Americans are not as loyal or patriotic as other nations. Nor is it true that our religion is defective in this matter. The error is not in our Protestant faith, but in our practice. The patriotism and lofty courage of our countrymen have been too often proved to need a word of defence. Nor should their piety be less conspicuous. I would not be misunderstood. I will yield to no man either in love for my country, or in zeal to keep the Church of Christ free from all alliance with party politics. It is very well known that I do not believe either in the divine right of kings, nor in the supremacy of the pope, the Czar, or any other potentate. I do not say, therefore, that any denomination of Christians should array themselves as a political party, and cast their votes for such candidates only as can pronounce their shibboleth. Nor do I say that our religious press and pulpits should engage in the political strife of the day. No; God forbid. All such things are, on every account, to be deprecated. All we mean to say on this point is, that men of acknowledged ability, and of sound principles and pure morals should be selected to administer the affairs of State, and that all Christians are bound to obey, honor and pray for their civil magistrates.

THE DUTY OF PRAYING FOR OUR RULERS.

1. We believe neither in the supremacy of the pope, nor in the divine right of kings; but we do believe that the *powers that be are ordained of God.* The heavens do rule. The Most High ruleth in the kingdom of men, and giveth it to whomsoever he will. Promotion cometh neither from the east, nor from the west, nor from the south. But God is judge; he putteth down one, and setteth up another. A man's heart deviseth his way: but the Lord directeth his steps. The lot is cast into the lap; but the whole disposing thereof is of the Lord. *Dan.* iv. 32; *Ps.* lxxv. 6, 7; *Prov.* xvi. 9, 33.

Statesmen and politicians may cast up crowns and play for kingdoms, and calculate upon their chances, and boast of their acumen and foresight, but Jehovah alone is King of kings, and the Most High alone is the supreme disposer of powers, princedoms and dominions. The flight of the tallest archangel before the eternal throne, and the immense sweep of comets and planets through the highest heavens are not more certainly directed by an Almighty hand, than are the evolutions of the sparrow. It is a hand almighty that crowns the angels with goodness and glory, and it is nothing less that paints the tulip and the rose, and feeds the young ravens when they cry. It is the all-seeing eye that directs the torch of discovery which philosophy bears round the globe, and kindles up on the outskirts of creation beacon lights for the advancement of coming generations; and it is nothing less that takes knowledge of the wants of the pious. The Lord knoweth them that are his. He approveth of their way. He numbereth the hairs of their head. His ear is ever open to their cry, his eye is ever upon them for good, and his hand is always stretched out for their relief.

The powers that be are ordained of God. That is, pious rulers are raised up as God's ministers for good; and wicked rulers are permitted as a scourge and chastisement for their people's sins. In the world we often see the poisoned chalice emptied by those who drugged it for others. *He that diggeth a pit falleth into it.* Haman's gallows for Mordecai was the instrument of his own execution. And often the very effort of our own evil thoughts—of the vaulting ambition of wicked men—

>——"O'erleaps itself
>And falls on t'other side"——

so it was with Pharaoh, with Nebuchadnezzar, and with Pilate, and with many others. Wicked men may be raised to power, and may propose to themselves mighty schemes by which to extend and concentrate their influence, and they may labor most perseveringly for their accomplishment, and with the consciousness of success walk in the palace of their imagination and say: "Is not this great Babylon, that I have built for the house of the kingdom, by the might of my power, and for the honor of my majesty?" But there is an overruling Providence, just and good, that guides, nevertheless, the wheels of the universe, and brings harmony out of the seeming chaos of human affairs. Pharaoh and Nebuchadnezzar were as truly the servants of God, in accomplishing his will, as Moses and Daniel. Surely the Lord maketh the wrath of man to praise him, and the remainder of wrath he restraineth.

> "There's a Divinity that shapes our ends,
> Rough hew them how we will."

The civil power, then, is in some sort the representative of the divine government. Our rulers are the image of the Divine Ruler. Magistrates are God's officers. To render them that respect and homage which is well pleasing in his sight, is to acknowledge his providence. It is an act of religious worship. It is an act of homage to God from whom all power emanates. It is an act of adoration. It is then a duty as well as a privilege to offer thanksgiving to Almighty God for our laws, liberties and institutions, and most worthy praise to his holy name for the warriors and statesmen, patriots and pious men that he has raised up for us, and to pray fervently for our rulers—for their personal welfare and the happiness of their families, and for the divine blessing to rest upon their official labors.

2. *To pray for our rulers is an act of true patriotism.* As it is our duty to reverence and obey them, so it is our duty to pray for them. No external form of respect can so fully demonstrate our affection for them, as the pouring out of the desires of our heart before the Lord for their welfare. Nothing can be a stronger argument of the esteem and consideration in which we hold them than the practice of praying for them. It is a practice without fee or emolument. It is difficult to conceive of any act so purely free from sinister motives, as the making of intercessions to Almighty God for our rulers.*

---

* "A foe to God was ne'er a friend to man." He that feareth not God regardeth not man. "As he who is not loyal to the king, can never well obey his officers, so he that subjecteth not his soul to the original power of his Creator, can never well obey the derivative power of earthly governors." "Magistrates are as truly God's officers as preachers; and, therefore, as he that heareth preachers, heareth him, so he that obeyeth rulers obeyeth him." See much more on this point, in Baxter's Works, London, 1830, vol vi. pp. 37, 38, *et seq.*

Nor is it surprising that even heathen princes should have required the prayers of their subjects in their behalf. Thus, in Ezra, we find a decree of the king of Persia, charging his officers to furnish the Jewish elders with sacrifices—all "that which they have need of, both young bullocks and rams, and lambs for the burnt offerings of the God of heaven; wheat, salt, wine and oil, according to the appointment of the priests which are at Jerusalem, let it be given them day by day without fail: that they may offer sacrifices of sweet savors unto the God of heaven, and pray for the life of the king and of his sons." *Ezra* vi. 9, 10.

And so, also, Pliny informs us concerning the Roman emperors, even in their heathenish state. "We have," says he, "been wont to make vows for the eternity of the empire, and for the welfare of the citizens, yea, for the welfare of the princes, and in their welfare for the eternity of the empire." *

---

* "Nuncupare vota et pro æternitate imperii, et pro salute civium, imo pro salute principium, ac propter illos pro æternitate imperii solebamus."—*Pl. Paneg.*

3. *Pious rulers, and all who acknowledge the Supreme Government of God, desire an interest in the prayers of their people.* And even those who seem not to feel their dependence upon the Sovereign Ruler of the universe, are pleased to have the people pray for them, for it is an act of loyalty that few will perform who are not sincere. It is a decent testimony of respect toward them, and greatly tends to establish their authority and secure obedience to their commands. How can we sincerely honor and reverence our rulers, if we have no heart to offer up prayers for them to him who has required us to pray for all men, especially for rulers and all that are in authority? It is the divine command, that ".every soul be subject unto the higher powers, not only for wrath, but also for conscience' sake. For, for this cause pay ye tribute also: for they are God's ministers attending continually upon this very thing. Render, therefore, to all their dues; tribute to whom tribute is due, custom to whom custom, fear to whom fear, honor to whom honor." It is, then, an act of patriotism, and of gratitude

and obedience to God, and of justice and charity toward our rulers to pray for them. How can we be faithful to our rulers, if we are not obedient "to the Most High, by whom princes rule and judges decree justice?"

If we sincerely and habitually pray for our country, we shall daily grow in attachment to it, and if we daily remember our rulers in our devotions we shall not fail to love and obey them. To neglect this duty is to be wanting in patriotism, as well as in obedience to the divine commandments. The best Christian is the best patriot, the most faithful subject, and the bravest warrior. A Christian is truly "the highest style of a man."

I exhort that—prayer be made for all men, for kings and for all that are in authority, that we may lead a quiet and peaceable life in all godliness and honesty.

4. *The piety and patriotism of praying for our rulers are seen in the practice of the Church of God in all ages.* The apostle's command in the text is positive. And it has been the practice of the pious in all past ages, and in all

countries to hold their civil rulers in esteem and to pray for them. It is a duty taught in the Bible, both by precept and example. God commanded the people by his prophet, when the Jews were conquered by the king of Babylon, and carried away captives, "Seek the peace of the city whither I have caused you to be carried away captives, and pray unto the Lord for it; for in the peace thereof shall ye have peace." The Scriptures abound in instances of the efficacy of prayer, both in regard to public and private blessings. Thus Abraham's prayer healed Abimelech and his family of barrenness; the prayers of Moses quenched the fire, and cured the bitings of the fiery serpents, and so of the prayers of Joshua, of Hannah, of Elijah, of Elisha, and of others. The prayers of Asa discomfited a million of Arabians, and those of Jehoshaphat destroyed a numerous army of his enemies by his own hands, and those of Hezekiah brought down an angel from heaven to cut off the Assyrians, and those of Manasseh restored him to his kingdom, and those of Esther saved her people from the brink of ruin, and those of Nehemiah inclined a pagan king's heart to favor his pious designs, and those of Daniel obtained for him visions, and the interpretation of dreams. Noah, Job and Samuel, and a host of saints have been powerful through much prayer, and as princes have prevailed with God. "All things," says the blessed Saviour, "whatsoever we shall ask in prayer, believing, we shall receive—He that asketh receiveth, and he that seeketh findeth, and to him that knocketh it shall be opened." "As the good bishop," says Dr. Barrow, "observing St. Austin's mother, with what constancy and passionateness she did pray for her son, being then engaged in ways of error and vanity, did encourage her, saying: *It is impossible that the son of these devotions should perish:* so may we hopefully presume, and encourage ourselves, that a prince will not miscarry, for whose welfare many good people do earnestly solicit; *Fieri non potest ut princeps istarum lacrymarum pereat.*" *

---

* Dr. Barrow's Works, vol. i., serm. x., p. 95. Et sic etiam "Si Stephanus non orasset ecclesia Paulum non habuisset."

It is a remarkable saying of a Jewish master, "Pray for the happiness of a kingdom or government; for if it were not for the fear of that, men would devour one another alive." And Josephus tells us, that "when the Jews were made subject to the Romans (though it was by conquest) twice a day they offered up sacrifices for the life and safety of the emperor." The apostle in the text directs that "first of all supplications, prayers, intercessions, and giving of thanks, be made for all men: for kings, and for all that are in authority." *Here is a positive command.* The Apostolic Constitutions, a very old work, though not the work of the apostles themselves, speaks of the prayers of Church, on communion occasions, for rulers. Tertullian assures us the "ancient Christians always prayed for all the emperors, that God would grant them long life, a secure reign, a safe family, valiant armies, a faithful senate, a loyal people, a quiet world, and whatever they as men, or as emperors, could wish. This they did," says he, "even for their persecutors, and often even in the pangs of the most cruel suffering and death."

Chrysostom says of the Christians of his time: "That all communicants did know how every day, both at even and morning, to make supplications for all the world, and for the emperor, and for all that are in authority." *

Lactantius saith to Constantine, "We with daily prayers do supplicate God, that he would first of all keep thee, whom he hath willed to be the keeper of things; then that he would inspire into thee a will whereby thou mayst ever persevere in the love of God's name; which is salutary to all, both to thee for thy happiness, and to us for our quiet." †

So Cyprian: "We pray to God, not only for ourselves, but for all mankind, and particularly for the emperors."

And Origen: "We pray for kings and rulers, that, with their royal authority, they may be found possessing a wise and prudent mind."

---

* For the originals of Tertullian and Chrysostom, see Dr. Barrow's Works, vol. i. p. 97.

† Lactant. vii. 26.

So, also, the ancient liturgies contain divers prayers for the emperors. And the confessions of faith and directories for public worship of all Protestant churches, recognize due obedience to magistrates and the duty of praying for them.

"We are to pray for the whole Church of Christ upon earth, for *magistrates*, and ministers, for ourselves, our brethren, yea, our enemies, and for all sorts of men living, or that shall live hereafter; but not for the dead, nor for those that are known to have sinned the sin unto death." *Larger Cat. ans. to* **183** *ques., and also the ans. to the* **127** *ques.**

5. It is but common Christian charity to pray for our rulers, *first*, because they are but men—our fellow men, and, *secondly*, they are more in need of our prayers than common men. "There are no men," says the late Dr. A. Alexander, "among us, who would be rendered more useful by Christian piety than those who are intrusted with power and official influence.

---

* See Vindications of Protestants in the point of obedience, etc. By Peter Du Moulin, D.D. An excellent work.

They are exalted above their fellow citizens, and should be exemplary in proportion to their elevation. Those who are delegated by the people to make laws for the protection of life, property and liberty, have an authority given them which is accompanied with a fearful responsibility. So few who engage in political concerns are governed by a regard to the glory of God, and the best interests of men, that the requiring that such would-be pious men, sounds strangely, and will appear unto many a novelty. That ministers of the Gospel, and other chief officers, should be religious men, all will admit, but that legislators and lawyers should be such, seems not to be evident. But there is no class of men in society to whom piety is more necessary and important than civil rulers. They need this ennobling principle to enable them steadily to pursue those objects which are connected with the public welfare."

There are some people who seem to think riches and titles, and offices of honor and trust, are vices of themselves, and that poverty and obscurity are much the same thing as godliness.

They presume on the goodness of God to give them eternal life in the world to come, simply because they have evil things here. They persuade themselves that all men above them are like the rich man in the Gospel, who fared sumptuously every day and was clothed in fine linen, but who died, and lifted up his eyes in hell, being in torment; and that they themselves are like Lazarus. As though God would send men to perdition merely because they were rich, and possessed of influence and standing among their fellow men, and save the poor and wretched merely for being poor. This class of individuals consider themselves as the supporters of the rich, whom they look upon as the caterpillars of society. To use their own style, the rich, or those intrusted with wealth and honors, live upon their labors, like drones in a hive; and salaried officers, whether in the state or the university, or on the bench, they consider as mice and vermin, that eat the honey which they, the poor laboring bees, have long been gathering. Such envious—I should have said wicked—thoughts are as far from truth, from just views of society and from the principles of the Bible, as they are evidence of a mean and contracted spirit. These very persons, by indulging such jealousies, show that the grapes are sour. They would act on the dog-in-the-manger principle if they could. They would themselves be what they suppose the rich and the great to be, if they knew how to attain such a condition. The most domineering and haughty are usually such as have been, by some freak of fortune, raised to wealth and power from humble circumstances. The most cruel masters are such as have once been slaves, but are now set over their *quondam* fellow-servants. The most haughty aristocrats—those that make the loudest pretensions—are often the merest upstarts. Families of the greatest pride are not unfrequently such as have once stood exceedingly low on the social scale. I am not objecting to every one improving his condition, if he do it honestly. I am not opposed to the apprentice becoming master, and the steward owner. I only mention these cases to show that the prejudice and ill will which the laboring classes are too prone to indulge against the rich, the learned, or the professional classes of society, are unjust, for there is no royal road to knowledge and power. The door is open to all. The highest gift of the freest nation on the globe may be obtained by the poorest freeborn man-child of America. These prejudices too, I am sorry to say, are proof of as much depravity in the laboring people, not as may actually exist among office-holders and the learned professions, but as they are supposed to possess. Those who are most apt to complain know not their own hearts. *Is thy servant a dog that he should do this thing?* And yet, says an old writer, "the dog did do that very thing." The bird flies high, but the arrow may bring him down; the fish swims deep, but the hook can bring it up: but the human heart, who can comprehend? It is an exceeding deep, who can find it out?

The Bible teaches us that riches and worldly consideration are not absolutely inconsistent with piety; but that it is more difficult for a man to be pious, who is encumbered with the possessions and honors of this world. This is perfectly obvious. Many of the pious men, however, named in the Bible, as Abraham and Lot, Job and David, were men of great wealth. Many kings and politicians, and lawyers and physicians, and philosophers and scholars, have been eminently pious men Such instances may be rare, but they are by no means impossible. Poverty is not always accompanied with godliness, but rather the reverse. *Godliness with contentment is great gain.* Rags and filth and sin, are much oftener found on the same person, than that a righteous man should be found begging bread. A man is not to lose his soul because he has estates, but for placing his affections upon them, and the neglect of his duty toward God and his fellow men. Nor is a man to be saved, because he is as poor as Lazarus, but because he is pious in his poverty. The Gospel knows no distinction of persons according to the flesh. All are concluded under sin. The same terms are propounded to all, whether rich or poor: namely, repentance toward God, and faith in the Lord Jesus Christ. He that believeth shall be saved, and he that believeth not shall be damned.

And as it is in grace, so it is in society. We are all members one of another. We are all parts of the same great web. We all have need of one another. I have need of you, and you have need of me. The happiness of each one is included in the well-doing of every one. Every one is his brother's keeper. In this great family there is, however, a great diversity of gifts and offices. *One is the head to do the thinking, and his thinking is really as much to the productive industry of the country, as the ploughing of the farmer. Another is the hand to do the working, and his working is as essential to the political and moral well-being of society as is the thinking of the other. And they are both equal.*

Our rulers, then, are doubly entitled to our daily intercessions at the throne of heavenly grace. They are *bone of our bone and flesh of our flesh.* They are our creatures. They are of us, but they are above us. Being of us, they are but men, fallible like ourselves. Being above us, they are by that very elevation the more in need of our charity and prayers.

First. Their duties are peculiarly difficult. The affairs which they are called upon to guide and settle are of great weight and importance, involving in their decisions the well-being of hundreds and thousands and millions of their fellow men. Measures of great consequence have to be examined, discussed, proposed, adopted. And even when there is much wisdom and ability and courage, and the purest intentions, it is not always an easy matter to hear a cause upon its true merits, and render a righteous decision. The burdens of office to a high-minded and virtuous man are never light. They that are great among their fellow men, are servants of all. Those possessed of estates and honors, talents and influence, are also possessed of vast entailed responsibilities. Nor can they escape from responsibility. It is as inseparable from them as their identity, and as lasting as their immortality. *He that increaseth knowledge, increaseth sorrow.* Much more does he increase his cares and labors that increaseth his riches and heapeth up honors, and runneth after and gaineth the homage of his fellow men. Our rulers are more to be pitied, to be loved and prayed for, than to be envied. "The world continually doth assault them with all its advantages; with all its baits of pleasure, with all its enticements to pride and vanity, to oppression and injustice, to sloth, to luxury, to exorbitant self-will and self-conceit, to every sort of vicious practice. Their eminency of state, their affluence of wealth, their uncontrollable power, their exemption from common constraints, their continual distractions and encumbrances by varieties of care and business, their multitude of obsequious followers, and scarcity of faithful friends to advise or reprove them, their having no obstacles before them to check their wills, to cross their humors, to curb their lusts and passions, are so many dangerous snares unto them; wherefore they do need plentiful measures of grace, and mighty assistance from God, to preserve them from the worst errors and sins; into which, otherwise, 'tis almost a miracle if they are not plunged." "All princes having many avocations and temptations hindering them to pray enough for themselves, do need supplemental aid from the devotions of others."—*Dr. Barrow.*

Second. They are exposed to peculiar dangers. As their field of labor is enlarged, so are the facilities for the gratification of appetite and passion increased, and the sources of temptation multiplied. And just as they are elevated above their fellow men and above their former condition in society, they are apt to forget their responsibility. Sometimes the height makes them dizzy. Sometimes even a trip to Washington makes our representatives forget their constituents and their kindred. Sometimes a voyage to Europe absolutely turns the heads of simple republicans. They come home full of lords and ladies, fetes and routs, and stars and ribbons and buttons, all such anti-American trumpery. Now their own dear native land grows nothing worthy of them. Their dress and china must be purchased in London or Paris. Alas, poor human nature! It is not every one of us that can bear elevation. He that can swim in his father's mill-pond, may be carried down with violence by the muddy turbulence of the great river. It is an observation of old Humphrey, that "like paper kites in the air, we do pretty well while checked with a strong string; but cut the string, and let us have our own way, and, like the poor kite, we come tumbling down into the mire." He that does very well with a thousand, may be utterly ruined by a hundred thousand. "It is harder," says some one, "for that bird to fly, that hath many pound weights tied to keep her down, than that which hath but a straw to carry to her nest. It is harder mounting heavenwards with lordships and kingdoms, than with less impediments." Even those that can bear an elevation to power are under temptations to make their license for doing whatsoever they will. Whereas, in fact, the greater power and authority any one hath, the less liberty he hath to do anything that is wrong or of questionable integrity.* For the greater the power and authority that God hath invested

---

* In maxima quaque fortuna minimum licere.—CICERO.

any man with, the greater are his obligations to be good himself, and to do good to his fellow men, because the greater is his influence and means to do good to others. The more influence a man's example has, the greater are his obligations to set a good one. What a delightful sight would it be to see those who are eminent in place and power continually setting an example of godliness! What would it not do for the moral character of our city, if all our authorities would *upon conscience* respect the Lord's day and the institutions of the Bible?

It will be admitted that those who are most worthy of our charities, are the proper objects of benevolence, and that it is our duty to pray for all men, then especially for our rulers, for they are *men;* and they are burdened with peculiar labors and trials, and exposed to peculiar dangers. They are like sentinels placed upon the top of a barren mountain, exposed to the merciless peltings of every storm for our safety, while we dwell quietly in the flowery vale below. The most fortunate of them have open enemies and insidious foes. They are surrounded by the jealous and the narrow-minded, or by disappointed office-seekers. Beset by the officious servility or parasites of flatterers, who soothe them in their faults, and humor them in their passions, and fire up their corrupt and vicious inclinations, whenever there is a possibility of advancing their own selfish designs. Exposed to violence and treachery, the cares of office, and temptations of place and power, who are so much in need of our prayers as our rulers?

Has not the ablest of them need to pray with Solomon: "Give thy servant an understanding heart, to judge thy people, that I may discern between good and bad; for who is able to judge this so great a people." It is not by mere human wisdom and strength that man prevails. The race is not to the swift, nor the battle to the strong. Salvation is of the Lord. "There is," says the psalmist, "no king saved by the multitude of an host." Except the Lord keepeth the city, the watchmen wake but in vain. Except the Lord preserve our laws and liberty and institutions, our army and navy, patriotic and brave as they are, will be but as chaff before the tempest.

Third. To pray for our rulers is then a duty to ourselves and our children, as well as to them and to the public. The good of the commonwealth is greatly affected by the principles and character of its rulers.

Where the people are the sovereign, rulers are the creatures of their will. The nation lives and has its breathing in its rulers. In oriental style a ruler is compared to a tall cedar, whose shadow is for protection and comfort; and his death is likened to its fall, that shakes the earth. That is, the death of a wise and virtuous ruler is a great public calamity. It is an interrupting of the regular administration of the affairs of state. It is a loss to the public of precious experience, well-tried abilities, patiently acquired confidence, and the consequent peril of putting public interest into hands untried. Hence King David is called the *light of Israel*, and hence the people once said to him out of the overflowing of their patriotic hearts, *Thou art worth more than ten thousand of us.* And so, also, Nehemiah and Daniel each complimented his sovereign by saying, *O king live forever*, which is translated in England into *God save the Queen.* As when the sun shines brightly the day is clear; as the ship is in good condition when out in open sea, with a good pilot, and sails crowded with prosperous breezes hastening toward the destined port, so the people are happy and prosperous when wise and good men guide the affairs of state. But woe to the land whose ruler is a child—weak, wayward, fickle.

The character and deeds of our rulers are inseparable from our national honor and prosperity. Our chief magistrate cannot say, *I am the State;* still, from the highest office in the nation's gift to the lowest, there is an inseparable connection between the national glory and the character of its rulers. The rulers and their electors are members of the same body. Their fortunes mutually reflect each other. The example, opinions and manners of men in office are the models of our young men who aspire to take their places. It is, therefore, of the most vital importance that they be pure-minded, upright men—men of good morals and sound principles.

The public welfare is essentially connected with the character and well-doing ot rulers. The honor and prosperity of rulers should be the glory of the people. They are inseparably united. The people cannot live happily if their rulers are in peril. They mutually partake of each other's fortunes. They make but one civil and political body, and what part soever of it suffers, all the other parts sympathize.

Thus Tertullian* says, speaking to Gentile magistrates, "We pray for you, because with you the empire is shaken: and the other members of it being shaken, assuredly even we, how far soever we may be thought removed from the calamity, are found in some place of the fall." The very same consideration the apostle introduces as the reason why we should pray

* Tertul. Apol., c. 32.

for our rulers, "I exhort you to make prayer for kings—that we may lead a quiet and peaceable life in all godliness and honesty."

The connection between the moral character and prosperous administration of rulers and the happiness of the people is obvious.

1. *From their influence upon the people.* Their example has great influence. "A king sitting in the throne of judgment scattereth away all evil with his eyes." "His power is the shield of innocence, the fence of right, the shelter of weakness and simplicity against violence and frauds. His very look is sufficient to advance goodness and suppress wickedness." The example of a pious man in power is a living law to the people, and does more than ten thousand statutes in precept alone, to mould and fashion public sentiment. The political opinions, the moral sentiments and the manners of civil magistrates are caught up, imitated and followed. If they are wise and good, sin is rebuked and the righteous are encouraged. If they are duellists and gamblers, if they are profane, Sabbath-breakers, neglecters of reli-

gion, licentious and infidel in their sentiments, and given to much strong drink, the pious mourn, and the wicked are emboldened in their iniquities.

2. *The influence of rulers upon the people is obvious from the close connection there is between their moral character and the happiness of the people.*

Righteousness exalteth a nation and establisheth the throne—when it goeth well with the righteous the city rejoiceth, for by the blessing of the upright the city is exalted. ·Ten righteous men would have saved Sodom. For the elect's sake, our Saviour informs us, the days of vengeance were shortened. The effectual fervent prayer of a righteous man availeth much. It is a munition of rocks for national defence. Now, since the Scriptures say so much of the piety of private persons, then how much more important is the example of pious rulers. Is it not said in the Bible that God, for David's sake, preserved Judah from destruction, even in the days of Hezekiah, when the king of Assyria invaded the land? God by the mouth of Isaiah declared: *I will defend the city of Jerusalem, for mine own sake, and for my servant David's sake.* Who can tell how often God has spared our guilty land for his servant Washington's sake, and for the sake of the Huguenot and Pilgrim Fathers, whom he winnowed out from Europe, and brought over to this then wilderness continent, to give it the Gospel, and to make it blossom and bloom as the garden of the Lord.

There are numerous instances in the Holy Scriptures which teach us that there is a moral connection of merit and guilt between rulers and their people. Mutually each is rewarded for the virtues, or punished for the vices of the other. For the people's sin sometimes misfortunes fall upon their ruler, and he is removed from them, or he brings upon them some calamity. Thus, Samuel said to the Israelites: *If ye do wickedly, ye shall be consumed, both ye and your king.* And so, on the other hand, for the sins of rulers, the people are afflicted. Thus Solomon's iniquities brought evil to all Israel. And so also in the case of David, when he numbered the people; and of Aaron, when he made the golden calf, and so also in regard to the sins of Saul and Jeroboam. And of Manasseh, it is said, *notwithstanding all the good deeds of Josiah, still the Lord turned not from the fierceness of his great wrath, wherewith his anger was kindled against Judah, because of all the provocations wherewith Manasseh provoked him. And Hezekiah rendered not again according to the benefit done unto him; for his heart was lifted up; therefore there was wrath upon him, and upon Judah and Jerusalem.*

We are too apt to impute all our misfortunes to our rulers, and take all our prosperity to ourselves. We often blame the administration of affairs, when we are ourselves chiefly in fault. Where, as happily with us, the people elect their own rulers, there the people are more to blame than the rulers. If they place over themselves a weak and wicked man, they become partakers in all his evil deeds. If they give power into the hands of a wicked man, they sin themselves, and they cause him to sin, and partake in all his sins. Where there is such sovereignty, there is a fearful responsibility.

3. It is our duty to do good to all men as we have opportunity—and to pray for all men; and, therefore, to do good to, and to pray for our rulers, for they are not stocks, nor stones, nor angels; but men—our fellow men, and the more in need of our prayers, as their labors and cares are increased. And to pray for our rulers is the cheapest, and yet the most effectual way of doing them good. However rich a man may be, he cannot dispense alms to every one; but he may enlarge his heart in prayer for the whole human race. "Our prayers can reach the utmost ends of the earth; and by them our charity may embrace all the world." By prayer the widow and the orphan may become benefactors to the rich, and the humblest citizen heap the choicest gifts upon the civil magistrate.

Since the breath of all men is in the hands of him who fashioneth and turneth their hearts whithersoever he will, it is our duty and privilege to pray to God to direct our rulers in the right way, and incline their hearts to what is well pleasing in his sight—that they may so administer justice with mercy as to secure peace of conscience and the approbation of the Judge of all—that in health and prosperity they may long live; and, finally, after this life, attain everlasting joy and felicity where all the pious shall reign as kings forever, through our Lord Jesus Christ. Amen.

It is then a plain duty enjoined upon all Christians to pray for the civil magistrate under whom they live. The character of the magistrate and the manner of reaching the high place of authority has nothing to do with the Christian duty of praying for him. It were difficult in the whole range of history to find magistrates more wicked and cruel than those actually in power, when the apostles wrote so plainly upon the duty of Christians to obey *the powers that be,* and to pray for those in authority. Historically also we have found it to be the teaching of the Church of Christ from its foundation, that Christians should pray for their rulers. And we do seriously call in question both the Christianity and the patriotism of any man that does not habitually pray for his country and its rulers. It is the divinely appointed economy that we should use means to obtain the divine blessing. And one of those means is prayer. Without prayer to God, we have no right to expect the divine blessing either upon ourselves or our country. If we call upon God, he has promised to hear us. *But the nation or people that will not serve him, he will destroy. The hand of the Lord is upon all them for good that seek him, but his power and his wrath is against them that forsake him. Them that honor me, saith God, I will honor, and they that despise me, shall be lightly esteemed.*

The man that lives without prayer lives in continual sin against his maker. And if he continue prayerless, he cannot go to heaven. And surely, if it is a Christian duty for all men to pray for their rulers, it is the duty of civil magistrates to pray for themselves and for the people. Parents and teachers esteem it a privilege to pray for those committed to their care. Much more should civil magistrates pray for themselves and for those over whom they exercise authority. *And whosoever shall call on the name of the Lord shall be saved.*

XIV.

CHRISTIAN SOLDIERS.

*Colonel Gardiner — Captain Vicars — Field-Marshal Suwarrow — General Havelock — General Jackson.**

WE allude again to Col. Gardiner, not to give any detailed account of his life. This is unnecessary, seeing that the history of his life and Christian character has long been familiar to the reading world. We would, however, have

---

* The author does not profess, of course, to give anything like an exhaustive notice of these distinguished warriors, nor to exclude many others from the right of being enrolled in a similar place in *The Church of the Army*. He has introduced these rather than others, because he was better acquainted with their history, and also because their characters seemed to him to be most fit illustrations of the main points in hand. The religious opinions of our own great WASHINGTON are too well known to need a remark. Indeed, it is believed that all our Great Captains are and have been believers in Christianity, and most of them communing members in the Church of Christ.

it distinctly remembered, that he was as well known for his love of country and for valor, tested in many a battle-field, as he was for piety. He was as brave and skilful in defending virtue against vice, and the truth of God against infidelity, as he was in leading his men into the thickest of the fight. During his earlier years, he often expressed a wish that it might be God's will for him to sacrifice his life in defence of religion and of the liberties of his country. This prayer was answered. The last record we have of him, written by himself, is in the following terms: "The enemy are advancing; but I trust in the Almighty God, who doeth whatsoever he pleases in the armies of heaven, and among the inhabitants of the earth. I have *one* life to sacrifice to my country's safety, and I shall not spare it." This was only the day before he fell beneath the blow of a broadsword in the battle of Preston Pans. The sublimest part of his life, however, was his example of godliness amid the profaneness and dissipation of the camp. Of Captain Vicars we have also spoken, and while we do not think his memoirs just the kind of a record that might do the most good, we do greatly admire the man as a Christian soldier. His lofty courage, self-denial, and diligence in doing good are ever to be remembered. He found time to pray and read the Bible, to visit the sick, attend meetings for prayer, and to cheer up his men amid the hardships and labors and perils of the camp as well as of the battle. We find him writing thus to his sister: "Be assured you will feel far happier in this world, even, by making religion your chief pursuit and study, than by all the pleasures and gaieties which your young heart may now be longing after. I tell you candidly and seriously, that I would willingly part with every earthly pleasure *for life*, for one hour's communion with Jesus every day!" And again: "Oh, that the Lord God would come among us with a high hand and with a stretched out arm; that he would, by the mighty power of the Holy Ghost, change and soften the hard hearts of those who despise the riches of his grace, and who make a mock of sin while standing on the verge of eternity;

that he would plant the rose of Sharon in all its freshness and fulness in the ground of every troubled, sin-laden heart." Such was the heart of the man, who gave his own blankets to his soldiers, and slept on leaves, and, like Jacob, had a stone for his pillow. Such was the Christian soldier, who roused his little band of two hundred in the dead of night to meet the attack of two thousand Russians in the trenches, by shouting: "Now, 97th, up and charge!" He himself led the way, and when a bayonet wound drew the blood copiously from his breast, his voice rose higher still, as he cried: "Men of the 97th, follow me!" as he leaped the parapet and charged the enemy. For a moment the moonbeams fell on his flashing sword as he waved it for the last time and gave his dying cheer to his men: "This way, 97th!" And he fell amidst his foes, but fell in the arms of victory.

FIELD-MARSHAL SUWARROW.

This officer is the greatest general Russia ever produced, and the most extraordinary man of his time. He combined the highest talents for war with the most extraordinary devotion. He had a superstitious influence over the minds of his soldiers. His deeds in arms are almost fabulous, and his manner of life singular. He had a philosophical contempt for dress, and might often have been seen drilling his men in his shirt sleeves. By exercise, cold baths, and frugal diet, which he always shared with the soldiers, he kept himself, even to old age, in a vigorous state of health. He was a rare example of temperance. He scrupulously kept all the fasts of the Greek Church. War and its duties were the whole occupation and diversion of his life. He inspired his soldiers with a courage that made them invincible, no matter how great the numbers or adverse the circumstances. He was a man of incorruptible honesty, immovable in his purposes, and inviolable in his promises. As he shared all the hardships and perils of his soldiers, so they never refused to follow him. He could march them farther, carry them through greater fatigue, and make them victors over greater odds, than any man in Europe. Devoutly religious, he would often stop his soldiers on their march for prayer or exhortation, and especially on Sundays, if opportunity offered, deliver them a lecture. He also obliged his captains to pray aloud before their companies, and abused those foreign officers who were not acquainted with the Russian prayers. To the love of his country he sacrificed every other sentiment, and consecrated without reserve all the faculties of his nature. So unbounded was the confidence of his soldiers in his sanctity and capacity to lead them, that they regarded him as the man chosen and sent by the Almighty to lead them to victory. Russian soldiers under him never surrendered, though surrounded by the enemy. They died embracing the image of their saints, which was attached as an amulet to their necks, but never surrendered. Of Suwarrow himself it was said, he "was never cold, afraid, nor defeated." For this estimate of this great field-marshal of Russia, we have relied mainly on Fowler's "Lives of the Sovereigns of Russia."

GENERAL HAVELOCK.

Among the Indian heroes of the British army, where shall we find a name more honored than that of Havelock, and where shall we find a character more like the Puritan, God-fearing ironsides of Cromwell? A late review, by no means fond of evangelical views, says of him: "His religion was no outward virtue, but a deep, living, all pervading principle, which was rooted in his very being, and tinged his whole character. He was one no more ashamed of praying than of fighting; but would sing psalms before all the army with as much courage as he would lead it to victory." His were the characteristicts of the true hero. An earnest religious conviction united with great military zeal and skill. His piety in no way detracted from his military duties. In the British army there was none more resolute or steadfast than Havelock. "And by a happy accident," says the Westminster Review, "there was allotted to him just such a duty as his soul loved. It was a time of sore trial for British India. The rebels were in the first flush of success. Regiment after regiment had fallen away from our standard. The British authority seemed to have dissolved all over the Northwest. In the lower provinces there were not more than some two thousand British soldiers to uphold our dominion. There was a general panic in Calcutta. It was then that Havelock was called to the command of the troops proceeding northward. The extraordinary series of efforts by which he retrieved our fortunes, beat back the torrent of revolt, wrought quick vengeance upon the fiend of Bithoor, and finally, after nine victories gained against armies numbering from ten to twenty thousand men, he succeeded in fighting his way, in spite of every obstacle, to the Lucknow Residency, and in averting its hourly imminent fall, is a portion of the history of this mutiny most familiar to the British public. In all this astonishing enterprise, pursued under the burning sun of an Indian summer, the great merit of Havelock is this, that with unflinching tenacity of purpose, he stuck to his one chief object—the relief of Lucknow. From the task which he set before himself at starting he never turned aside. Onward, with iron steadfastness, he urged it through all hazards; onward, through rain, sun and fever; onward, through countless hosts of a desperate enemy, with the motto—'Remember Cawnpore—Remember the ladies!' No knight of romance strove more earnestly for the Holy Grail—no Crusader more stubbornly pursued his sacred pilgrimage."

Havelock waited long for the work of his life. "Toiling painfully and obscurely for nearly half a century of the best years of his life, the work came at last to him which he was to do. He did it and died. He lived to see the crowning of his noble purpose, but not to receive the full meed of his country's approbation. The brave spirit had worked out its puny tenement, and sped to the God of its faithful service. Since the death of Nelson and of Moore, never death of any man has excited in England such wide and deep sorrow—a sorrow

almost domestic in every English home."—
Westminster Review on Indian Heroes.

Havelock was remarkable for his diligence, sobriety, strength of intellect and soldierly bearing, as well as for his piety. When compelled to remain inactive, in the daily routine of camp or post duty, he spent his time in the study of languages, of military science and the history of war, in the discipline of his troops and in the religious instruction of the men under his charge. He devoted himself so successfully to the study of Oriental languages that he became military interpreter in the British army in Persia and Burmah. It is obvious that one of the great evils of the military service is the idle time that hangs on the hands of young officers, at isolated or remote posts. But it is within their power to turn all their time to advantage. Havelock passed nearly half a century in preparation for the crowning events of his life. Twelve years between the Burmese war and the Affghanistan war, he spent in the daily routine of military duties. But he lost no time. For it was then that

Oriental languages and the science and history of war, and religious literature and the work of Christian missions occupied his time.

Havelock was proud of his profession and loved active military service. The profile view of any such man must therefore be manifestly unjust. We must take a full face view, reconciling as well as we can his Christian character with his deeds as a warrior; and to do this we have first decided that the profession of arms is not in itself sinful, though we believe almost all wars are unjustifiable, wicked and unnecessary. But we do not see how a subaltern officer or a private is any more guilty for serving in an unjustifiable war than the citizens who pay taxes to support it. And besides, who is to decide on the character of a war? Is every private to sit in judgment on the war before he consents to obey orders and fight? This is subversive at once of all government. The powers that be are to be obeyed by Christians in going to war as in other things, except where their commands are clearly contrary to the commandments of God. So the early

Christians understood the Gospel precepts on this subject. Some of the best soldiers in the armies of the pagan emperor of Rome were devout Christians. They considered it their duty as Christians to pray for them and to fight for the empire.

General Havelock's greatness of character, then, seems to us to have consisted of his strong common sense, vigorous intellect and abiding religious impressions from early youth. The religious training of his mother is seen in all his career. The child of six years under his father's roof in Kent was father to the man and to the hero dying in India. The man of sixty was seen in his boyhood as through an inverted telescope. His military greatness was not a mere chance. Nor was it the growth of an hour, but the ripe fruit of a lifetime of severe study, of self-denial, of self-government, obedience to orders, strict temperance, and of arduous service for his country, both in the camp and in the field. He was himself an example of what he wished his men to be. A most rigid disciplinarian for the drill, and in action he *led* his men through the most stirring scenes with the coolness and accuracy of a parade drill. The foundation of his great success was laid in the fearlessness of his course and in the open, honest, full-heartedness of his religious faith. "It was not in Havelock's nature to hide his colors. His uniform did not more fully declare his profession as a military man, than did his uniform Christian conduct, his position in the church militant." "His enlistment was as hearty under the banner of the Lion of the tribe of Judah as under the lion of Britain. He is an illustrious example, both from the lustre of his name and the lustre of his course, and from the dark sky out of which his star shone so steadily in its undimmed, ever-increasing brilliance."—*Boardman's Higher Life*.

"Come and see how a Christian can die. I have so ruled my life for more than forty years, that when it came I might face death without fear. I die happy and contented. Thank God for my hope in the Saviour. We shall meet in heaven." "I am not in the least afraid. To die is gain. I die happy and contented." And his last words were to his loving son, who had shared with him the perils of the battle-field, "Come," said he, "come, my son, and see how a Christian can die."

Such is the end of an upright and pious man. In death tranquil, confident, hopeful, joyous. Such is the end of those that live a life of faith upon the son of God, rejoicing in Christ Jesus, but without any confidence in the flesh.

GENERAL JACKSON.

"There gleams a coronet of light around our hero's brow."

Our sketches would be sadly defective without a reference to General Andrew Jackson. Pliny, in his letter to Atrius Clemens, says that he had "an opportunity to look into Euphrates, the philosopher, being frequently at his house, and that he knew him to be a shining example of polite learning." It was our privilege for a considerable time to know General Jackson, and to be often as guest and pastor in his hospitable mansion, and even share his own private cham-

and not in vain, for missives of love. And General Jackson's ardent attachment to his wife, and reverence for his mother's memory, is proverbial. Not long before his death, he said: "Heaven will be no heaven for me, if I do not meet my wife there." No man loved little children more fervently, nor enjoyed the bliss of the family circle with greater satisfaction. He never seemed more happy than with one of the little ones of his household on his knee, or in his arms. His favorite recreation, as long as he was able to mount his horse, was to take one of the little children before him on the saddle and ride over his farm.

Now what such men as Vicars, Hammond, Jackson and Havelock have done, others should imitate. Indeed it seems to be a law of our nature, that great men who are loving and pure, tender and affectionate at home, are as bold and fearless as lions abroad or in the defence of their country and the inmates of their homes. The names we have given prove the possibility and illustrate the imperative duty of maintaining religious principles in the camp as well as at home, and show that soldiers should preserve the conjugal and parental relations untarnished even to the ends of the earth, or the utmost bounds of the ocean.

2. These cases illustrate, *that mere human virtues are not to be substituted for repentance toward God and faith in Jesus Christ.* Virtuous and patriotic in the highest sense, unselfish, benevolent, kind, forgiving, temperate, truthful, sound-minded and right-hearted, and full of deeds of greatest courage, yet faith in Christ was added as the only way of salvation. We have found Cornelius believing with all his heart upon Christ as soon as he is preached to him, and submitting himself to the righteousness of God. And so did Havelock and Jackson. They believed in Christ and depended upon him alone for salvation. By faith they were justified and their sins forgiven. They were accepted in the Beloved, and made complete in Christ. Their example says, depend not upon loyalty, patriotism and courage, nor upon more than Roman virtue. Be a good father, a good neighbor, a faithful and tender

husband, a good citizen, but depend not upon these things for justification in the sight of God. When you are all these, you have no merit at all. You are still a sinner against God, and must accept of pardon through his Son Jesus Christ. You must take him as he is offered in the Gospel, a prophet, priest and king, a complete, all-mighty, willing Saviour. "The blood of Christ," and "the merits of atoning blood" and "the sufferings of the Son of God for us sinners," were favorite expressions of both Havelock and Jackson.

3. We learn from these cases, *that opposition to religion, and even persecution for our faith, must not cause us to deny it.* Joseph of Arimathea, the centurions of Capernaum, of the Crucifixion and of Cesarea, were under peculiar temptations to deny Jesus; but they felt their obligations to him to be paramount to all others. Nor are our modern military heroes wanting in moral courage. Whenever Havelock's convictions of duty were ascertained, no sarcasm, nor contempt, nor sting of the scoffer, nor charge of fanaticism, or of pietism, could

move him from doing his duty. Obedience to God was his highest standard. It was his constant effort to preserve a conscience void of offence toward God and toward man. And when he was reproached with being a fanatical Baptist, a ranting Methodist, a pietist, the Governor-General of India examined the charges, and was so delighted with the discipline and influence he had over his men, that he said he wished to God Havelock had baptized the whole army.

And General Jackson not only always maintained a high regard for the Bible, the Church and her ministers and ordinances, but he was always ready to avow his convictions in their behalf. He was never ashamed of the catechism of his mother, nor of the religion of his wife. "The holy Sabbath," said he, "is ordained by God, and set apart to be devoted to his worship and praise. I always keep it as God's holy day. I always attended service at church when I could."

4. Let us learn, wherever we are, or in whatever profession or business we may be, *to try to*

do good. One centurion we find building a synagogue for the Jews at Capernaum; another, Cornelius, giving alms to all the people, and another saving the life of Paul and other prisoners from the violence of the soldiers. And at the Shivey Dagoon of Rangoon and on the beach after a shipwreck, and on the tented field and at Jellalabad, and at Cawnpore and Lucknow, we have Havelock always a *confessor* for Christ, and fervent in his prayers and efforts to make him known to his soldiers. And when but a subaltern, we find him sacredly devoting one-tenth of his entire income to religious purposes. Though one of the bravest of the brave, and one of the most active soldiers for forty years, spent in camps and armies, in marches and sieges, he always found time for prayer and the reading of God's holy word. And so also the church at the Hermitage was built, and rebuilt and kept up chiefly by the contributions and influence of General Jackson. He was not only generous as Hâtem in his hospitalities, but his purse was always open for the support of ministers of the Gospel. He never was appealed to in vain for the poor, or for aid to support the worship of God. Generosity is closely allied with bravery.

5. These histories teach us to be *catholic in our feelings.* The learned professions and the studies and pursuits of military and naval science, travel and acquaintance with mankind have a tendency to liberalize our ideas, but this is perhaps preëminently so with soldiers and sailors. In the almsgivings of Cornelius, the synagogue built at Capernaum for the Jews by a Roman centurion, and the kindness of Julius toward Paul, we have instances of victory over national prejudices and all narrowness of mind. Now while we have no sympathy with indifferentism or latitudinarianism, we do hold it to be a high Christian duty to love and fellowship all who love our Lord Jesus Christ in sincerity. We have no sympathy with an exclusive, intolerant bigotry. Wherever the spirit of Christ is, there we acknowledge Christ himself; and we know that if we have not the spirit of Christ we are none of his. A happy instance of the catho-

licity of General Havelock is found in his fellowship with the Presbyterians of the Free Church of Scotland at Bombay, with the members of which he delighted to worship. "He took a part in their prayer-meetings, and his hand and purse were both open to assist them in carrying out their various plans for the education and religious instruction of the natives. Havelock was wholly destitute of that narrow sectarian prejudice which impairs the excellence of so many even true Christians. *He communed with all evangelical denominations, and regarded creeds as of small consequence compared with true piety.* Once in a meeting at Bombay, this question of denomination being referred to, he explained fully and freely his views. Though he 'should part,' he said, 'with his Baptist principles only with his life, he was willing cordially to fraternize with every Christian who held by the Head, and was serving the Redeemer in sincerity and truth. And here he would protest against its being alleged, as adversaries would insinuate, that when men of various denominations met, as this evening, in a feeling of brotherhood, they could only do this by paring down to the smallest portion, the mass of his religion; on the contrary, he conceived that all brought with them their faith in all its strength and vitality. They left, indeed, he thought, at the door of the place of assembly, the husks and shell of their creed, but brought into the midst of their brethren the precious kernel. They laid aside, for a moment, at the threshold, the canons, and articles, and formularies of their section of Christianity, but carried along with them, up to the table at which he was speaking, the very essence and quintessence of their religion.' "—*Headley's Life of Havelock.*

Such feelings we believe are common with enlightened minds, but especially so with brave men. They love piety better than creed. No man disliked petty jealousies and narrow sectarian feelings and denominational shibboleths more cordially than General Jackson. Though a Presbyterian by birth, education, conviction and preference, both as to doctrines and modes of worship—as to faith and church order and government—still his views on religious subjects were truly broad and catholic. No man was more ardently devoted to religious freedom, nor more tolerant of the rights of conscience.

6. Let us learn that no circumstances, however unfavorable to pious efforts, are a sufficient excuse for neglecting personal religion. The Roman centurion of Capernaum and of Cesarea were remarkable for their attention to their households. Their education, position, and profession were much in the way of their devotion to God, yet we find them overcoming every obstacle. And surely no man could have greater turmoil and care than Havelock had in Affghanistan and Oude, yet his religious habits were kept up without intermission. He was not a day without his Bible, and often engaged not only in silent prayer, but in its outward act. It was a special object with him, somehow or other, to be left alone both morning and evening, that he might bow down and worship God. He was constantly at church or chapel whenever an opportunity was offered. The

first thing everywhere with him was the kingdom of God and his righteousness. His whole life, and his death declare that "where there is a will to serve God, there is a way." Vicars and Hammond also found time for much pious meditation upon God's Word. And we have seen also that General Jackson was never without his Bible, and always attended church when he could. Surely, then, the distractions of business, the urgencies of a learned profession, and even the anxieties of the tent and of the battle-field, are no excuse for neglecting the one thing needful. What has been done may be done again—may be done by American soldiers.

The speaking dead, the voices from glory, all

———" Remind us,
We can make our lives sublime,
And departing, leave behind us
Footprints on the sands of time—

"Footprints, that perhaps another,
Sailing o'er life's solemn main,
A forlorn and shipwrecked brother,
Seeing, shall take heart again.

"Let us, then, be up and doing,
With a heart for any fate,
Still achieving, still pursuing,
Learn to labor and to wait."

THE END.